OCCUPATIONAL CHOICES, NETWORKS, AND TRANSFERS

OCCUPATIONAL CHOICES, NETWORKS, AND TRANSFERS

An Exegesis Based on Micro Data from Delhi Slums

ARUP MITRA

MANOHAR
2003

First published 2003

ISBN 81-7304-483-X

Published by
Ajay Kumar Jain for
Manohar Publishers & Distributors
4753/23 Ansari Road, Daryaganj
New Delhi 110 002

Typeset by
Kohli Print
Delhi 110 051

Printed at
Print Perfect
Delhi 110 064

To my teachers

K.L. Krishna and Edwin S. Mills
and
the have-nots

CONTENTS

PREFACE

The volume focuses on issues relating to strategies that individuals from low income households develop in order to overcome risks, particularly in the urban job market. Their major aim is to face the challenges, and, accordingly, they respond by pulling together their resources, both economic and social. Networks and transfers are the manifestations of links that individuals develop in helping each other. Slums appear to be the dark spots on the city contours but a detailed analysis reveals that they actually represent the 'triumph of the human spirit over poverty and want'.

'To do good work one must eat well, be well housed, have one's fling from time to time, smoke one's pipe, and drink one's coffee in peace.' (This was the view of Van Gogh, which he communicated to Emile Bernard in September 1888.) When one faces persistent deprivation of the minimum consumption requirements, doing good work is certainly not possible. Hence the impact of widespread poverty on economic growth is phenomenal, though this relationship often remains unrecognized. This justifies the role of the State as far as the investment in the social sector is concerned because the empowerment of the poor can be best attained through education and health. Their individual efforts to escape poverty can be strengthened by State support.

The present study analyses occupations, earnings, and the standards of living of the low income households, and their strategies and efforts to overcome uncertainties about employment, expenditure, and housing. Networks and transfers (both monetary and non-monetary help)—which can be based on either pure altruistic behaviour or the principle of exchange (mutual help)—take the central position in the analysis. The other major aspect refers to the interspatial variations in economic activities performed in the city and their impact on the segmentation of the labour market, which influence the occupational choices, earnings, and the standards of living of the slum inhabitants.

The database of the study is drawn from the micro survey on slum households conducted during 1999–2000 in different parts of Delhi.

The survey was carried out by the Institute of Economic Growth, Delhi, while financial support was provided by the World Bank, Washington, D.C. (Development Research Group: Dr V. Rao and Dr M. Woolcock) under the project, 'urban poverty, social capital, and risk management'. The questionnaire was prepared by the members of both teams. Comments from colleagues, friends, and anonymous referees enriched the work in several ways. In particular, I would like to thank Dr Satish Deshpande, Dr Indrani Gupta and Professor Kanchan Chopra. I am grateful to Dr Alakh N. Sharma who offered extensive comments on an earlier version of the draft. The chapter on women in the informal sector is based on the paper commissioned by the South Asia Social Development Unit of the Bank, with the financial support from the Innovation Fund of the Gender Anchor. I am grateful to Dr Karin Kapadia for this.

Thanks are due to Mr Devmani Upadhyay for his excellent research assistance. Dr Deb Kusum Das offered advice at all levels. My mother has been a constant source of inspiration, encouraging me to work on the problem of slum dwellers. Finally, I need to acknowledge the infrastructure support I have received from the Institute of Economic Growth, Delhi in preparing the study.

ARUP MITRA

CHAPTER 1

INTRODUCTION

The rapid spread of slums and squatter settlements in large Indian cities evokes an image of extreme poverty. Though some of the residents of these slum clusters in due course have moved up the social ladder in terms of their standard of living, a large majority of the inhabitants continue to reside in conditions of acute deprivation, denied healthy and safe shelter, sanitation, sewerage, and drinking water. All this may be seen in terms of an outcome of uneven industrialization and unequal economic development, leading to the building up of immense pressure on both land and housing. However, the slum dwellers should not be considered merely the victims of dire poverty, but should also be seen as dynamic agents capable of implementing their own economic strategies and of finding appropriate responses to the challenges posed by specific urban environments (Dupont, 2000).[1] It is interesting to note, as the following chapters will reveal, that many slum dwellers have evolved strategies to cope with the uncertainties and risks relating to employment, income, shelter, and health, and have thus behaved in the most rational way under their given circumstances. The success stories of upward income mobility—be it within the same broad occupational category or across occupations—suggest that informal mechanisms of networking help individuals adjust to their changing needs, aspirations, and problems. Hence, rather than regarding the entire issue of slums as the outcome of certain macroeconomic forces, it would be helpful to understand the behaviour of the slum inhabitants as a rational response to the changes occurring around them. This shift in focus will in turn provide inputs to the formulation of policy that would recognize and respect both the role of the state (as a facilitator) and the role of an individual agent in maximizing his/her welfare. The scope for unnecessary interference by the state and hence an increase in social cost would then be minimized, and at the same time the coexistence and optimal combination of both individual strategy and state participation would reduce the possibilities of the exploitation of one individual by another. This would in turn also determine the degree of commercialization that would be beneficial for the society. In other words, the domains of state and individual action based on altruism and/or exchange (market) can be defined clearly to serve the greater common interest.

The literature on the 'new' urban economics explains the existence, size, and structures of urban areas, viewing cities as market responses to opportunities for production and income (Mills, 1967). Economies of scale induce businesses to concentrate the large-scale production of goods and services in one place. The cost of moving goods and services induces producers to locate near other producers with whom they make exchanges. The high cost of moving workers between dwellings and work places induces employers and employees to locate near each other. Finally, technology is generated and diffused rapidly if producers those who have similar technologies and face similar technical problems locate near each other. Keeping in view the availability of resources, different activities emerge in different parts of the city. The literature on localization economies views the city as a specialized centre of a particular industry/activity (Henderson, 1986). But the literature on urbanization economies takes a more realistic view in suggesting the coexistence of different activities within a particular city (Mills, 1967), and the city benefits from the simultaneous existence of different activities, a large overall labour market and a large service sector interacting with manufacturing (Mills, 1967). Hence, strong urbanization economies may lead to the development of diversified large areas, whereas localization economies foster specialized metro-politan areas if these economies occur in combination with the possibilities for inter-area trade. The impact of information and communication technology on human settlement has manifested itself in what is called a 'divided city': new landscapes of innovation, economic development, cultural exchanges, political dynamics, and social inequalities within cities and urban regions are emerging (*Global Report on Human Settlements*, 2001).

In response to the growth of diverse economic activities, employment opportunities of various types emerge in different parts of the city. And the job seekers in accordance with their skills and capabilities respond to such opportunities and changes occurring within the city. In an attempt to reduce their commutation cost they settle in and around their work place, which in turn exerts pressure on land and housing. Their ability to organize themselves and the political clout that they may exercise determine the provision of basic amenities by the local government in areas which were never meant for human habitation in the first place. Hence, the growth of slums and low income households is indicative of several forces that work simultaneously to shape and influence the complex process of urbanization. The proliferation of slums illustrates the relationship between the transformation of urban space, population movements, and social re-composition, which are all important factors affecting the urbanization process and city planning.

The responses of individuals to economic opportunities available are again indicative of the various subtle mechanisms that they adopt in the process of maximizing their earnings and ensuring their own welfare. The networks, which are not truly exogenous, of course, constitute a significant component of this job search process (Chopra, 2002). The socio-economic and cultural factors determine the nature of the networks to which an individual takes recourse; the nature of the networks also changes with the rise in the duration of the migration, employment experience, and the acquisition of marketable skills. The entire process of upward mobility demonstrates the interplay of several socio-economic and cultural variables, which again in the context of urban transformation keeps changing to give rise to a spectrum of new processes as substitutes for the older ones. Though in the first instance the nature of the network decides the occupation that an individual will choose or will engage in, the nature of economic opportunities (occupations) also determines subsequently the nature of the network that an individual will decide to adopt in implementing his or her future job market strategies. Issues relating to occupational choices and networks are so complex that any empirical question in this regard remains far from being completely answered. Caste-kinship bonds, education, infrastructure, and indivisibilities all intermingle with each other and shape human behaviour with elements so diverse that a framework based on any single academic discipline finds it impossible to satisfactorily explain them.

In this context, issues relating to gender are again of major importance. Not only is the discrimination against women labour in the informal sector of interest to scholars but one also needs to know, how low income households share their responsibilities and distribute resources among the household members. The standard of living analysis, based on poverty measures in terms of household or population below the poverty line, is far from being able to capture the reality. Opportunities, earnings, contributions, and intra-household distribution of resources, therefore, all need to be discussed in the broader context of gender.

It is interesting to note that some of the issues relating to networks and access to job opportunities are actually part of the much larger issues that address themselves to individual action—altruism and/or exchange—manifested in terms of transfers—monetary and non-monetary both—across households. A society with a majority of individuals with altruistic motives would be Pareto superior to a society which did not hold the virtue of altruism in high esteem. But at the same time a society which valued altruism to a small degree may be far inferior to one with pure exchange (Stark, 1995), because in such cases the possibility of exploitation in the name of altruism may exist. Hence, the extent to and the area in which altruism and exchange are followed need to be understood by the state in order to minimize the possibilities of individual exploitation and at the same time allow individuals to enhance their welfare. In other words, excessive state intervention may undermine or weaken the institutions and the mechanisms that individuals might have evolved to cope with the uncertainties they face in their daily struggle for survival. For example, an extreme step taken by the state to clear the slums can be both a costly affair as well as counterproductive. The provision of space, amenities, and transport for resettling the slum inhabitants elsewhere, or for creating employment opportunities in the rural areas to discourage in-migration to the city, may also turn out to be a costly affair. On the other hand, the demolition of slums without looking into any of these alternatives would not only be unjustified on humanitarian grounds (being anti-poor), but would also prove to be harmful for the economy, as mentioned earlier. That would mean destroying the informal networks and strategies which the low income households might have developed to escape deprivation. Disallowing the workers to pursue their activities in the urban informal sector would also reduce the volume of output and services produced in the economy; in addition, this would also cause social tensions relating to unemployment and increase the suffering of an increasing number of people.[2] Further, it may be argued that an individual has the right to work, and, hence, there is no justification for the dismissal of his or her self-initiated activities without providing for suitable alternatives.

Keeping in view the urban problems of developing countries, much concern has been expressed regarding the spatial allocation of population and the size distribution of cities. One of the major worries is that big cities in the developing countries are too large or are growing too rapidly, leading to fiscal and administrative unmanageability, regional income inequality, political unrest, and considerable urban disamenities including crime, pollution, and congestion. In the Indian context, a great deal of government action (based not on much serious economic analysis) revolves around the issues concerning optimum city sizes and the desirability and effects of programmes to control city sizes (Mills and Becker, 1986). The anti-urbanization view, in fact, reached its peak in the declaration of the 1974 World Population Plan of Action at Bucharest. But all this seems to be one-sided, ignoring the individual actions and strategies adopted to deal with the problems associated with unemployment, underemployment, and poverty. It also overlooks the employment opportunities and the productivity-augmenting effects that cities generate in the course of their growth, and the role of cities as engines of economic growth and social change. The present volume, based on a primary survey, aims at bridging this gap in the literature by analysing the following issues:

(a) the occupational choices of the slum dwellers and the roles of different types of networks in accessing information pertaining to the job market against the backdrop of diverse economic activities conducted in different parts of the city;
(b) the changing nature of networks, occupations, and upward income mobility patterns with a rise in the duration of migration in the city;
(c) determinants of the standard of living of the slum population, judged not only in terms of per capita expenditure but also their access to basic amenities and their health conditions;
(d) transfers based on individual actions in terms of altruism *versus* exchange, which enables them to formulate strategies and take recourse to networks for the betterment of their economic conditions; and
(e) the contribution of women to the household economy notwithstanding the discrimination they face in the informal sector.

These issues have been analysed in Chapters 3, 4, 5, 6 and 7, respectively. Chapter 2, explores the conceptual framework regarding the formation and growth of urban slums. It is important to note that the issues discussed in Chapters 3 and 7 are not entirely independent of each other, but for the sake of convenience they have been discussed separately. A review of government policy in the Indian context, and the conclusions of the study are presented in Chapters 8 and 9, respectively. The detailed layout of the chapters with discussions on the data and the sampling framework appear at the end of the next chapter.

NOTES

1. Dupont (2000) gives a detailed account of some issues affecting the pavement dwellers in Delhi.
2. Both Banerjee (1986) and Mitra (1994) explore this theme, suggesting the relevance of the informal sector in the context of employment generation.

CHAPTER 2

GROWTH OF SLUMS: A FRAMEWORK

This chapter lists some of the important factors behind the growth of slums in cities. Though the focus here is primarily on economic issues, some of the social and political conditions that encourage the formation of slums are also noted. The list is not exhaustive; it is merely suggestive. Second, the defining characteristics of slums as adopted in various surveys and/or studies are also discussed. Finally, we present the outline of the sampling framework which we followed in conducting the survey of slum households in Delhi on which this study is based.

2.1 Factors Influencing the Growth of Slums

AGRICULTURE

In developing countries, particularly those with a predominant agriculture sector employing more than 60 per cent of the national workforce, the agricultural situation largely determines the decision of rural populations to migrate to cities—crop failure and fall in per capita availability of land and/or food accompanied by a sharp rise in rural destitution usually prompt rural-urban migration. This is at least what the traditional literature on this issue had us believe ('overurbanization' thesis; Hoselitz, 1953, 1955). The argument has, however, been significantly altered in other studies both from the analytical and empirical points of view. While one class of literature envisaged a direct relationship between the rise in agricultural productivity and the surplus labour willing to migrate to cities (Lewis, 1954) in order to take advantage of the rural-urban income differentials (Harris-Todaro, 1970), another class of literature argued in favour of the inability of the rural destitute to migrate to the urban areas (Banerjee, 1985). Rather, the middle-income households in the rural areas are said to reveal a greater propensity to migrate than their counterparts in the top- or bottom-income size classes. A corollary of this proposition is that there would not necessarily be a one-to-one correspondence between migration and urban slum formation; at least the degree of association would be less compared to the situation suggesting the outflow of the rural destitute on a large scale.

RURAL NON-FARM SECTOR

With rapid agricultural growth, it is possible to create an economic environment for occupational diversification as put forward by the Lewis approach (1954). But then, agricultural productivity is not a sufficient condition for rural industries to emerge; other supply side factors also matter, such as infrastructure, marketing facilities, credit, technology transfer, and skilled human capital.

An increase in agricultural productivity can raise non-agricultural employment either by raising the demand for non-agricultural products and services or by displacing labour from agriculture (due to mechanization), which leads to its residual absorption in the non-farm sector. From a simple positive association between the two variables it may not be safe to suggest clearly the existence of a demand linkage, though in the context of the rural industries, in particular, a positive association between its performance and agricultural productivity could be taken as the positive impact of rising purchasing power and resources generated in the agriculture sector for further investment in the non-agriculture sector (see Papola, 1987). On the whole, the non-farm sector is said to engage two different categories of labour: (a) those who are pushed out of the agriculture sector but who are not able to migrate to the urban areas, resulting mostly in the residual absorption in the rural non-farm sector, and (b) those who shift to the non-farm sector in response to a rising demand for their services. The former may be described as a repository of surplus rural labour, and the latter may be seen as comprising demand-induced employment (Mitra, 1993; Acharya and Mitra, 2000).

The Harris-Todaro (1970) model argued that in the face of expected rural-urban income differentials population outflows from the rural areas will take place until wages are equalized across space. For the rural poor in particular, the expected income differentials are much larger than those for the non-poor, and hence by implication the rural poor have a higher propensity to migrate. As already mentioned, Banerjee (1986), however, argues that those in the middle-income group migrate largely because the rural poor cannot afford the cost of transfer, and the high-income households are not required to migrate in search of jobs. Our argument here is a bit different: from the rural non-farm sector eventually both the groups, mentioned earlier, migrate to urban areas although for different reasons. Those engaged in low-productivity activities strive to reach the urban areas in subsequent years in search of better employment opportunities. Even when they are located in petty activities, the income in the non-farm sector is usually higher than what they could manage to earn when engaged in agricultural activities, and this provides for their subsequent transfer to the urban areas. Quite clearly a two-stage process is involved in their occupational mobility: in the first stage, they are pushed out of the agricultural sector in which they engage in marginal activities, and enter the rural non-farm low-productivity activities, and in the second stage they seek an entry into the urban job market using their previous job experience and the resources generated in the process to overcome the rural-urban discontinuum. On the other hand, earnings from demand-induced activities in the rural non-farm sector are large enough to offer them incentives to undertake more risky ventures in the urban areas, with an expectation of larger incomes accruing in the future. Successful enterprises in the rural non-farm sector prefer to shift their location with a view to catering to a larger market, which may enhance their profitability. However, this does not mean any significant upward mobility in terms of housing conditions until at least they manage to secure stability of income. Often they arrive in slums in the cities, though within the slum community itself several types of clusters based on amenities available and housing materials used for construction can be identified. Depending upon their liquidity situation migrants develop access through networks to these various categories of slums.[1]

RURAL AREAS IN THE NEIGHBOURHOOD OF THE URBAN AREAS

Non-farm employment, particularly the employment in the manufacturing sector in the rural areas, is taken to vary positively with urbanization (Shukla, 1991). This is partly because dispersal of industries in the rural areas around the periphery of the big cities may be attributed to certain factors, which are related to urbanization. For example, diseconomies of agglomeration, measures adopted for controlling environmental pollution, escalating land prices in the city and problems of labour organizations in large urban centres lead to the spillover of urban-based activities to the nearby rural areas. In the initial stages the positive externalities of the concentration of activities are significant but as population inflow speeds up, congestion and overcrowding outweigh the economies of scale. In such a situation the solution for the new entrants is to invest in the areas in the periphery of the big cities. This enables them to tap the land resources available at reasonable prices and at the same time develop access to the existing infrastructure within the city. Subsequently these villages start producing commodities and services quite similar to those produced in the urban localities and which tend to get integrated into the national market (Kundu, 1992). On the negative side, agricultural land is increasingly used for non-agricultural purposes. Apart from the loss in agricultural produce that is one of the outcomes of this process, population also tends to concentrate in such areas, resulting in what is popularly called 'rurbanization'. Such semi-urban localities, because of the lack of adequate and appropriate infrastructure, are not suitable to the rapid growth of population and other productive activities, and eventually deteriorate into slum clusters. Common property resources which were formerly sufficient to support the rural population which resided there before the momentum of this process had picked up, now find that it cannot meet the pent-up demand subsequent to the new growth that takes place in these areas. In explaining the growth dynamics of slums in cities, these components cannot be ignored because of their heavy dependence on the city infrastructure. Although these semi-urban centres do not, strictly speaking, fall into the domain of city municipal/metropolitan limits, they do account for a significant part of the expanding new areas of the existing urban centres.

URBAN INFORMAL SECTOR

Economic development brings about a shift in the structure of value-added activities/products as well as a shift of the workforce away from the agriculture sector towards the secondary and tertiary sectors. Developments in the agriculture sector resulting in an increase in labour productivity reduces the share of agriculture in the total workforce, and, with a rise in per capita income, the demand for non-agricultural products also increases, thus causing a shift away from agriculture towards the manufacturing and the tertiary sectors in terms of value-added. Any major deviation from this line of development or, in other words, a mismatch in production and workforce share implies gross productivity differentials across the sectors. A large share of agriculture in the workforce but with a moderate share in the total value-added implies moderate productivity levels in this sector, and a sluggish rate of labour productivity implies a declining land-man ratio as land supply is almost fixed in the face of a rapidly growing population, and therefore the labour force.

Deterioration in the land-man ratio, as the 'overurbanization' thesis holds, pushes labour out of the agriculture sector. And urban in-migration in the face of a limited spread of industries and/or sluggish employment growth therein—resulting from a distortion in the factor market and other technological reasons—forces them to land in the urban informal sector. Though the urban informal sector is highly heterogeneous in terms of the nature of its activities, and, therefore, it may be quite misleading to comment on productivity in this sector, in general it is characterized by low productivity and hence meagre earnings. The cause of low productivity, however, could be significantly different for different activities, ranging from technological reasons to many others. In the case of own-account manufacturing enterprises it is usually the lack of reproducible tangible capital which forces the units to adopt inferior technology, resulting in low productivity. On the other hand, self-employed households engaged in trading and related activities are often too many in number, which tends to reduce their bargaining power and leads to the distress sale of products. The wage-labour-dependent households usually do not have access to regular employment; besides, the situation of excess supplies reduces the wage rate, particularly in service-related informal sector activities. Meagre earnings force these informal sector workers to reside in slums, as they are left with only nominal resources after meeting their consumption requirements. Hence, considerable overlaps between households below or marginally above the poverty line, slum residents, and informal sector workers are quite evident in the cities of the developing countries.

INDUSTRIALIZATION

This is not to suggest that slum dwellers are essentially engaged in the informal sector only. In many of the industrialized cities workers employed in the high-productivity industries also live in slums primarily due to shortage of housing and space.

Due to their spatial concentration non-agricultural activities reap the advantages of the external economies of scale, which can broadly be categorized into two groups: urbanization economies and localization economies. The former implies that activities of different types benefit from concentration, while the latter points to the concentration of similar activities. Localization economies, as Henderson (1986) describes, reflect (i) economies of intra-industry specialization where greater industry size permits greater specialization among firms in their functions, (ii) labour market economies where industry size reduces search costs for firms looking for workers with specific training relevant to that industry, (iii) scale of communication among firms affecting the speed of adoption of new innovations, and (iv) scale in providing the public intermediate inputs tailored to the technical needs of a particular industry. The urbanization economies, on the other hand, as mentioned above, are external to both firm and industry, and result from the general level of economic activity in that city or an increase in the total city population. A large city is said to benefit from a high level of economic activity in that city, a large overall labour market, and a large service sector interacting with manufacturing (Mills, 1967). While strong urbanization economies may lead to the development of diversified large areas, localization economies foster specialized metropolitan areas if these economies occur in combination with the possibilities for inter-area trade. By implication firms in large cities are usually characterized by higher levels of technical efficiency, and also experience rapid technological progress.

Concentration of economic activities occurs mainly to reap the advantages of externalities arising from indivisibilities in the production process such as the interdependence of industries in terms of input-output linkages, ancillarization, marketing of products, and availability of infrastructural facilities. The 'development pole' theory explains how other groups of industries tend to form clusters around a core of industries, which have a high capacity to transmit growth impulses through both backward and forward linkages. Such clusters are said to form industrial complexes, the advantages of which are as follows (Hermansen, 1972): (a) substantial economies of investment expenditure—the investment for the whole complex is less than the sum of investment for each enterprise planned and located in isolation, (b) efficient production due to the advantages of specialization, economies of large-scale operation, and organization of common managerial and infrastructural facilities, (c) possibility of co-ordinated exploitation of the natural and raw material resources of the area of location, and (d) opportunities for close contact, rapid diffusion of technological innovations, and rapid overall development of the economy.

But such external economies of scale tend to get dissipated as concentration of population and demand for infrastructural services exceed the existing facilities. A point arrives beyond which the diseconomies of scale outweigh the economies of scale to such an extent that the cost of living in terms of land and material cost, for example, becomes enormous. Even when wages are much above the minimum consumption requirements housing remains almost unaffordable. In such a situation several organized-sector workers engaged in high-productivity industrial and tertiary activities are also forced to stay in slums. Evidence from Mumbai slums highlights this fact (Mitra, 1990).

Another disadvantage in such industrialized cities is the constant flow of migration from the rural areas. The very existence of the high-productivity sector in these cities attracts migrants, as the rural-urban development disparity appears to be phenomenal. Even when the probability of getting high-wage employment is low, the inflow of rural population still continues, as the urban informal sector may appear attractive when compared to the job opportunities available in the rural areas and other small urban settlements. But the cost of such growth may be envisaged in terms of the proliferation of slums.

The presence of interdependent and indivisible infrastructural facilities leads to the concentration of a large spectrum of economic activities in cities. This raises the land value and rents, thus limiting the access of a large section of the population to reasonably decent dwellings. Economies of agglomeration being strong in the industrialization process, particularly in the early stages of development, the absence of planning creates giant megalopolises with a low quality of life (Datta-Chaudhuri, 1980). The relatively older dwelling units deteriorate into slums (*pucca* slums) due to overcrowding and shortage of basic amenities, though at the time of the construction they were not so. In such situations not only the informal-sector workers with low incomes but also several formal-sector workers with earnings much above the poverty line may also reside in slums. In several industrialized cities, as mentioned above, the formal-sector workers reside in slums as they cannot afford better-quality housing in spite of unionization, which protects their incomes at a considerably high level relative to other consumption requirements.

NETWORKS AND THE DESIRE TO RESIDE NEAR ONE'S WORK PLACE AND RELATIVES

Having briefly examined some of the macro variables controlling the growth of slums in cities, we now turn to individual and specific elements that contribute to slum formation. Migrants from rural areas, particularly those from low-income households, reveal a strong preference to reside near their work place. The network/contact factor plays a significant role in not only offering them jobs but also in providing shelter and other necessary resources and skills for settling down and surviving in the city. As the jobs obtained through contacts are quite similar to those of the contact persons, the later arrivals such as the co-villagers, relatives, kith and kin, and friends show a strong tendency to live near the early settlers. And thus overcrowding increases not only in the place of settlement but also in the domain of the work place. In other words, in relation to certain activities slums and low-income households grow rapidly in certain parts of the city.

The very nature of the activities which the migrants perform sometimes acts as the motivating factor for residing near their work place. The self-employed workers engaged in petty manufacturing and repairing activities often run their enterprises within their household premises, as observed by Sethuraman (1976). Besides, workers engaged in trading activities are required to use their work place for residential purposes mainly from the security point of view. Often these workers encroach upon public land to run their businesses; the constant fear of demolition by the local government prompts them to reside near their work place. Similiarly, the provision of community toilets and drinking water near the marketplace also induces many workers to dwell close to their work place.

It is also noted that members of low-income households often perform more than one/two job(s). In particular, women who combine their household activities with jobs outside the home prefer to have their place of work and their place of residence close to each other. Domestic maids, for example, work in a large number of households, performing more or less similar kinds of work. For them the distance between the place of work and home is a significant factor in deciding their allocation of time within and outside the household. Even if the total income earned from all jobs located close to their residence is less than the income which they could earn from a job available at a distant place, the women would prefer the former option as long as the cost of commuting and the opportunity cost of the time spent on commuting are large enough to reduce their expected income from the job at a distant place. In his survey of migrant households in Delhi Banerjee (1984) noted that even a majority of the workers who entered the informal wage sector—relatively speaking the most unstable sector both in terms of the lack of regular jobs and steady incomes—did not pursue their job search after they had obtained their first jobs.

Other than economic factors, sociological and political factors also influence the decision of rural migrants to reside in the neighbourhood of relatives, friends, and co-villagers. The migrants are anxious to anchor themselves physically, economically, emotionally, and psychologically in their new urban environment by drawing on their own cultural resources. This desire for the comfort and security of the known as a counter to the anonymity of the metropoliton experience encourages the new entrants to the city to congregate and live and work with their own compatriots and fellowmen. Physical proximity to one's caste members, co-villagers, relatives, and friends cushions the initial shocks of city life and eases their transition. In India, the multilingual and multiethnic identities of its citizens make such adaptations even more important. Thus, the more culturally and ethnically heterogeneous an area/country is, the more likely it is that migrants would seek to settle in and around the areas already claimed by their brethren. Besides, as mentioned above, since the activities of the contact persons (early entrants) and the late entrants are mostly similar, the sharing of family or individual resources in their pursuit of economic goals becomes almost inevitable. Efforts to delay slum demolition programmes planned by city administrators, and the attainment of quasi-permanent residential rights in the city are realized only through the collective efforts of the rural migrants which help secure patronage from politicians and ward bosses in exchange for their promise to operate as vote banks.

Having noted the importance of personal contact in securing employment and the desire to reside in groups formed on the basis of caste-kinship-co-villager bonds, and the preference of the low-income migrant households to locate near the work place, we now turn to the development of various nodes (centres) within the city, each characterized by specialized activities. As the literature on agglomeration (particularly the localization) economies suggests, firms conducting similar activities tend to locate close to each other in order to reap the economies of scale (Henderson, 1988). Extending this argument—usually made at the inter-city level to explain the differences in the activities in whch cities specialize in—to the intra-city level, the heterogeneity across space even within a specific city can be noted. In other words, not all areas would conduct all activities—each area would be responsible for the growth of a predominant activity depending upon the availability of resources required for its generation. Thus different centres within a city would be home to specialized activities, though from the point of view of the overall city all activities would appear to exist within its territory, thus creating the myth of a vast labour market. Empirically also the heterogeneity of the city structure across space has been documented; the study by Dupont and Mitra (1995) divided the city of Delhi into several small units—census charges—and observed wide interspatial variations of socio-economic characteristics and activities. Further, they also found an incidental matching of these socio-economic variables with geographic zones of the city; while certain attributes were more conspicuously present in certain zones, others were absent in other zones. All this tends to suggest the diverse nature of the city's socio-economic structure.

In addition to the desire to stay near the work place and one's relatives, we may also note that the preference patterns of certain individuals as manifested in their consumption patterns may reveal a strong bias against housing. Often migrants turn to poor quality housing at low prices in order to use their limited savings to purchase other consumer durables in the long run and to meet other urgent needs and immediate responsibilities in the short run. Hence, the growth of slums to some extent is inevitable, particularly in the face of rising prices.

POLITICAL VOTE BANKS

Ending poverty through the empowerment of the poor has been a much discussed proposition. Several government and non-governmental organizations have emerged to combat poverty through various strategies particularly in the age of globalization. Several international donor agencies have extended substantial support to organizations working in this field of poverty alleviation. The term demolition of slums has become almost obsolete; local governments now speak of the possible relocation of clusters, a policy which is difficult to execute. Even in the 1960s and 1970s slum demolition programmes proved to be quite ineffective as the slums once cleared often re-emerged in other parts of the city. In addition, political parties have their own vested interests. Increasingly they use slum populations as vote banks, and in exchange bestow at least a semi-legal right to the land on which the slum diwellers encroach, and also grant them ration cards. When rural migrants arrive in the city, they seek the comfort of a collective identity based on caste, kinship, and village of origion so that their entry into the competitive, alienating, harsh and disorienting urban environment may be eased. Political parties often offer these preconditions of comfort and security.

MALFUNCTIONING OF THE HOUSING MARKET

The housing market involves serious distortions. Government agencies and city development authorities have not been able to increase the supply of housing, and as a result demand has exploded. Speculation in the land and housing markets has raised property prices to exorbitant levels. The acquisition of a large component of the housing constructed by city development authorities by a small percentage of potential buyers for speculative purposes has resulted in further corrupting the housing market.

Authorized private builders offer prices which are as high as those in this parallel housing market, and thus for a large section of the population housing remains unaffordable. On the other hand, it has become a lucrative business for a few speculators who are engaged in the sale and purchase of immovable property.

By providing undue protection to tenants rent control acts encourage the deterioration in the quality of housing and discourage property owners from making any further investment in the maintenance of the existing units. All these factors have a severely adverse effect on the growth of low-quality housing and slums.

REMITTANCES

Even when some individuals can afford better-quality housing, they prefer to reside in slums because they remit a significant part of their earnings to their villages and homes. Remittances or the transfer of resources can be explained only partly but not wholly in terms of altruism. As Strak (1995) points out, the transfer of resources is also prompted by self-interest. In order to prevent the further entry of relatives, kith and kin, and co-villagers into the highly competitive and unstable urban job market, which has a strong tendency to reduce urban wages by increasing the supplies of labour, migrants decide to remit a share of their earnings on a regular basis. Even if the possibility of a wage cut is ruled out, the migration of relatives means that the early settlers have to provide certain amenities to the later entrants. And the cost of providing shelter, food, and employment could be large enough to induce the early settlers to work out means of keeping their relatives away. Remittances viewed from this angle offer a very different interpretation of the issue. And this factor could partly explain why some people prefer to stay in slums even when they gain access to better jobs and higher earnings in due course.

2.2 Defining Characteristics of Slums

The definition of a slum varies from study to study, which reflects the different perceptions and meanings of the term as understood by scholars and policy makers and ultimately this influences slum populations. In general, the term is used to describe mud structures, overcrowded dilapidated dwelling units, and so on, and it 'has long had a negative connotation, has been almost an epithet implying something evil, strange, to be shunned and avoided' (Clinard, 1970). However, slum dwellings do not simply constitute the slum economy nor does the emergence of a few mud structures and overcrowded houses shape the slum society. Clinard (1970) argues that a slum involves much more than the elements of inadequate housing, deficient sanitary and hygienic facilities, overcrowding, and congestion by which the term is generally understood: 'Sociologically it is a way of life, a subculture with a set of norms and values which is reflected in poor sanitation and health practices, deviant behaviour and characteristic attributes of apathy and social isolation.' For the purposes of quantification, however, some working definition of a slum is warranted as the definition quoted above involves many non-quantifiable factors.

In 1956, when the 'Slum Areas (Improvement and Clearance) Act, 1956' was enacted initially in Delhi and thereafter in 11 other states, a well-defined set of attributes was attached to the term 'slum'. The

Act defines slums as 'areas where buildings (a) are in any respect unfit for human habitation; (b) are by reason of dilapidation, overcrowding, faulty arrangements of streets, lack of ventilation, light or sanitation facilities, or any combination of these factors are detrimental to safety, health or morale'.

The working definition of a slum employed by the Bharat Sevak Samaj (1958) in Delhi was as follows:

> The term 'slum' should be applied to those parts of the city which may (on the face of it) be considered unfit for human habitation either because the structures therein are old, dilapidated, grossly congested and out of repair, or because it is impossible to preserve sanitation for want of sanitary facilities including ventilation, drainage, water supply, etc., or because the sites by themselves are unhealthy. (Bharat Sevak Samaj, 1958)

The above definition was wider in scope as it was not simply confined to the hutments but old dilapidated buildings unfit for human habitation were also included in the survey. So *katras* (or 'slum tenements, constructed normally in rows, within a compound or enclosure having a single common entrance') along with *bastis* (described as 'a thick cluster of small kutcha houses or huts built on open land, often in an unauthorised manner') were taken into account.

The same type of definition was also suggested by the Commissioner of the Madras Corporation in 1961, where not only slum hutments but also overcrowded buildings in a state of deterioration were said to form slums.

'So the term "slum" will also include such dwellings which on account of such overcrowding, dilapidation and lack of ventilation are detrimental to safety, health and social morale' (*Census of India*, 1961, Madras).

However, the 1961 census, though it adopted this definition while estimating the slum population in the city (Madras), excluded the other categories of slums, i.e. dilapidated buildings, dwellings lacking ventilation, etc., referred to by the Commissioner.

The survey of the Bombay Municipal Corporation in the late 1950s (cited in Desai and Pillai, 1972) also considered tenement slums as defined above, and not only the huts, while defining a slum. The survey adopted a three-fold classification of slums: (a) *Chawls*: Areas with permanent multi-storeyed buildings built long ago according to the standards then prevailing, but which are today in a deteriorated condition.[2] (b) *Partrachawls*: Areas with semi-permanent structures both authorized and unauthorized often built of corrugated iron sheets and commonly known as 'patra-chawls', *patra* meaning tin sheet or some such material. (c) *Zopadpattis*: Areas commonly referred to as squatter settlements, shanty towns, or hutment colonies, consisting of hovels made of a variety of hard and soft materials such as pieces of wood, rags, tin sheets, mud, bricks and any such thing that comes in handy.

Apart from such a classification of slums as tenement slums and hutment slums, another categorization has also been applied especially in the context of the bustees of Calcutta. Some bustees in Calcutta are known as 'registered slums' when they are recorded in the assessment books and the Calcutta Corporation collects taxes from them. 'To qualify for registration, the total area must not be less than 1/6th acre, and the structures must be kutcha, that is, they should have a roof built without cement, with not more than 18" of the wall of pucca construction' (Singh and D'souza, 1980). On the other hand, the slums which do not meet these structural criteria are called 'unregistered slums'. The Calcutta Metropolitan Development Authority referred to such a classification of slums while estimating the slum population for the year 1974 (Singh and D'souza, 1980).

The scheme Environmental Improvement of Urban Slums (EIU in short) came into operation in 1972 and thereafter received much attention under the Minimum Needs Programme and the 20-Point Programme; it gained much popularity during the years 1983–4 and 1984–5. The EIU defined a slum in the following words:

> A slum area means any area where such dwellings predominate which by reason of dilapidation, over-crowding, faulty arrangement of design of building, narrowness or faulty arrangement of street, lack of ventilation, light or sanitation facilities, inadequacy or open spaces and community facilities, or any combination of these factors, are detrimental to safety, health or morale. Any slum area selected for improvement under the scheme should have at least 2/3rd of the slum families in the poor and low-income groups with an income of less than Rs. 250/- per month. Also, there should be no likelihood of any slum clearance or redevelopment programme being taken up in that area for a period of at least 15 years in case of pucca built slums and 10 years for hutment type slums, so that adequate benefit is secured from the money spent on improvement.

The first part of this quotation referring to the definition of a slum resembles that of the 1956 Act described at the beginning of this section. In addition, the income criterion has been added in this definition of a slum. The terms used in these definitions as 'factors detrimental to safety, health or morale', however, sound quite subjective and this element of judgement indeed poses a difficulty in identifying a slum. Over and above, it appears that usually the following twin criteria are taken into account in most of the definitions for identifying a slum population: (a) physical convenience and (b) the type of structure. Although from a sociological point of view, a slum has been defined as an areal unit and not simply as a single neglected dwelling unit, no matter how bad its condition might have been (Bergel, 1955) and, also, has been described as 'a way of life' (Clinard, 1970), such characteristics are not always reflected in the working definition of a slum as examined above.

We have referred to a few definitions adopted in different surveys for estimating a slum population. The main purpose has been to indicate that the scope of the definition varies from study to study. However, it needs to be mentioned that this section is not exhaustive; against the backdrop of a large number of definitions of a slum available in the literature, we have selectively discussed a few to reflect its wide variability. Given this variability it is futile to look for objective and definitive estimates of a slum population. Since the nature of slums in different cities is not homogeneous, a uniform and objectively operational definition is not possible. Even within the same city different definitions would result in different estimates of slum populations (see Mitra, 1994).

This study is based on the list of slum colonies (*jhuggi-jhonpdi*) prepared by the city development authority. It may be noted that the list provided by the Delhi Development Authority is neither comprehensive nor exhaustive. Various illegal/squatter settlements and marginal settlements located in different parts of the city are not necessarily covered by this list; the primary focus is on registered slums. Structures constructed temporarily by the short-duration migrants are less likely to be covered in this survey; rather, slums which are stable in nature and have received recognition by the city development authorities have been included. The defining characteristic of these slums refers to an area and a group of households located therein—*katcha* and semi-*pucca* households with inadequate provisions for sanitation and/or drinking water. The detailed socio-economic survey conducted by the National Sample Survey Organisation on slum dwellers in 1976–7 also referred to a similar kind of definition (Mitra, 1994).[3] As mentioned above, both from the sociological and the economic points of view a number of households located across an area reveal certain characteristics in terms of which they may be termed slums. A single household existing in isolation cannot be considered as a slum even if in terms of housing characteristics and basic amenities it falls into the same category. From this point of view, most of the definitions discussed above share a common criterion, though in terms of the coverage of area and the recognition received from city/municipal authorities they could be different, thus resulting in different estimates of slum populations.

2.3 Sampling Framework

The database of the study is drawn from the survey carried out for 802 households in 30 slum clusters in Delhi in the year 1999–2000, over a period of six months. The slums considered in our study, as mentioned above, are only of a particular type: the *jhuggi-jhonpdi* colonies given in the list prepared by the Delhi Development Authority (DDA). A brief description of the sampling procedure followed to select the 802 sample households is given below.

In order to select the 802 sample households we have used a three-stage stratified random sampling framework. Based on the DDA list of 456 slum clusters, each with at least 200 households, we decided to select 30 clusters. This survey comprises two components: one is qualitative and the other is quantitative in nature. The qualitative survey was carried out in three clusters, two from south Delhi and one from north Delhi. As we intended to include all these three clusters in our quantitative survey as well, we followed the random sampling technique to ultimately select 27 clusters only.

(i) In stage 1, clusters each with a population of 200 households were distributed across 7 zones in Delhi.

(ii) The proportion of the number of clusters in each zone Cz (z = 1...7) to the total number of clusters across all zones, C was taken as the weight to arrive at the distribution of 27 sample clusters across the 7 zones. The number of clusters to be picked up for sampling, let us say, is Xz.

(iii) The next step concerns drawing the Xz number of specific sample clusters from the Cz number of clusters located actually in a zone. All the Cz number of clusters in each zone with their detailed addresses were codified and put in a box from which

Xz number of draws were made. Xzi stands for a specific cluster in zone Z. The process was repeated for all the seven zones, separately.

(iv) Once the specific clusters from each zone were identified, the distribution of 754 sample households was made using the proportion of the number of households in each cluster (HHXzi), to the total number of households in all 27 clusters (HHX, where X = sigma Xz), as weights. To this we added 48 households selected from the 3 clusters, 16 each, where the qualitative survey was carried out.

(v) In each of these clusters, investigators prepared a list of households with some identifiable characteristics based on which we drew a lottery to pick the specific households for the detailed interviews enabling us to fill in the quantitative questionnaires.

2.4 Organization of the Study

Keeping in view the issues delineated in the first part of this chapter, the organization of the study is as follows:

Chapter 3 deals with the occupational choices of the slum dwellers, highlighting the role of networks in accessing jobs and the segmented nature of the urban labour market. The term labour market segmentation here refers to the physical segmentation due to the growth of specialized activities in different parts of the city. In Chapter 4 we assess the occupational mobility of those who migrated from the rural areas. The frequency of change in occupations and improvements attained, if any, are analysed in this chapter. Chapter 5 refers to the standard of living of the slum dwellers, and Chapter 6 deals with remittances and transfer of resources across households referring to issues such as altruism and exchange. In fact, links among individuals or households, which are broadly manifested in terms of networks as discussed in Chapers 3 and 4, would remain incomplete without a discussion of inter-household transfer of resources. Gender discrimination in the informal sector is the focus of Chapter 7. Though some of these issues could have been taken up in Chapter 3 itself, for the sake of convenience and for keeping the size of each chapter within reasonable limits, we prefer to present gender-related labour market issues separately in Chapter 7. Policy issues are discussed in Chapter 8, and finally, the major findings are summarized in Chapter 9. All these aspects taken up in different chapters are interrelated and basically fall into the domain of the labour market and standards of living within the broad context of networks and transfers. No attempt has been made in this study to analyse the secondary data (NSS and population census) on slum dwellers, partly because they have already been analysed in great detail in our earlier studies (Mitra, 1990, 1994; and Gupta and Mitra, 2002).

NOTES

1. Even when they physically do not migrate, the concentration of non-farm activities leading to the concentration of population transforms the civic status of the place from rural to urban, and often these areas, being close to the existing larger urban settlements, tend to form part of the expanding city limits.
2. This type of slum is possibly unique to Bombay.
3. The results of this survey are analysed in Mitra (1990 and 1994).

CHAPTER 3

URBAN LABOUR MARKET: NETWORKS AND PHYSICAL SEGMENTATION

3.1 Introduction

Studies on the urban labour market have confirmed extensively the role of contacts in accessing information pertaining to jobs in both formal and informal sectors. Banerjee's work (1986) on the urban labour market and migrant households in Delhi brings out the importance of the rural-based search for urban jobs through contacts. These contacts operate through relatives, friends, members of one's caste group, and co-villagers. About half of Banerjee's sample of migrants seem to have migrated only after pre-arranging a job or after receiving assurance of employment from an urban-based contact. As job expectations were guided by information received from urban-based contacts, migrants were in general successful in obtaining their desired employment in the first instance. This could be one of the important reasons why a large majority of the migrants did not continue their job search after joining their first job in Delhi. Even those employed in the informal sector did not continue their search on any large scale. Although migrants who entered wage employment in the informal sector were twice as likely as those who entered the formal sector or those who were engaged in non-wage employment to continue their search after accepting their first urban job, a large majority of even those who entered wage employmet in the informal sector did not continue their search thereafter. And non-wage workers in the informal sector were no more likely than entrants in the formal sector to keep searching for jobs (Banerjee and Bucci, 1994; Banerjee, 1983, 1984, 1991).

It is interesting to note that migrants whose contact persons were engaged in unskilled manual occupations were informed about the same job more frequently than those whose contacts worked in non-manual and in skilled manual occupations (Banerjee, 1984). Further, migration undertaken at the suggestion or behest of contacts appeared to be important among those who were illiterate or who were non-matriculates. While matriculates moved with the security provided by pre-arranged jobs, graduates relied predominantly on formal channels to pre-arrange their jobs.

Another major feature of these studies on the urban labour market is that caste, income from first job, landownership, and sector of first job are quite important factors in explaining the job search by rural migrants, though among urban migrants they are not as important (Banerjee and Knight, 1985; Banerjee and Bucci, 1994). Scheduled caste migrants displayed a greater propensity than non-scheduled caste migrants to pursue on-the-job searches for employment in the formal sector but not in the informal sector. This is primarily due to the reservation policy applicable to the scheduled castes in the formal sector.

On the whole, the assumptions of the probabilistic models that the job search is entirely an urban-based activity and that employment in free-entry activities is a means of financing the search for high-income or high-productivity jobs have been challenged. Other studies have revealed the importance of contact variables in rural-urban migration and the rural-based search for urban jobs, which could also be largely in the informal sector instead of being confined to the formal sector alone. Below we examine some of these points in more detail.

Ever since the advent of the probabilistic models, issues of rural-urban migration in developing countries have invited both theoretical and empirical research. As mentioned above, it is by now widely acknowledged that rural migrants access information on the urban labour market through various informal channels, and tend to experience an upward income mobility by migrating to the urban areas. However, one missing area of research has been the segmented nature of the urban labour market due to specialization of activities in different areas (zones) within a city. Segmentation along the lines of caste, skill, and education has of course drawn adequate attention from scholars, but the physical segmentation of the urbon labour market is an issue which has received relatively less attention. By physical segmentation we mean the inaccessibility of certain kind of jobs to certain group of individuals, primarily because of the distance factor within a city; (high-income jobs may be available in a particular locality, but its physical distance from the place where one specific group of migrants resides in the city could be so enormous that such jobs may remain inaccessible to them). Even inexpensive (intra-city) transport for commutation need not eliminate these urban labour market barriers, especially in developing countries. Hence, occupational choice is greatly determined by the narrow spectrum of jobs available within the geographic area where the migrants reside, rather than by what they are capable of pursuing. Contact-based migration tends to end up in providing jobs in neighbourhoods close to their residence; the early settlers help their relatives, friends, members of their caste groups, and their co-villagers to migrate to the city by providing information on jobs and spaces in which to settle down, which are often in the same field and in the same activities to which they themselves have access. As a result, occupational choice is more or less supply-driven, though from the macro point of view—keeping the entire city in perspective—the equilibrium choice of occupation would be the outcome of both demand and supply-side factors. It is also in sharp contrast to the popular interpretation of informal sector employment, namely the supply (of labour) push phenomenon. This perception is further substantiated by the fact that intra-city differences (across space) in terms of development, infrastructure, and activities are too significant to be ignored. This chapter explores part of this aspect while also analysing the occupational patterns and earnings of low-income migrants in the city of Delhi.

The existing literature, as mentioned above, on rural-urban migration, is vast and controversial. The 'over-urbanization thesis'—perhaps one of the oldest theories—holds that with the deterioration in the land-man ratio in the agricultural sector, the rural population, in search of a livelihood, migrates to the urban areas (Hoselitz, 1957). Subsequently, in the face of limited possibilities of labour absorption in the organized sector, particularly in industry, the rural migrant workers are believed to create a situation of unlimited supply of labour in the urban labour market. This leads to a residual absorption of labour in the informal sector, which is generally said to comprise activities characterized by low productivity. Besides, the subsistence levels of income accruing to workers in this sector inflate the percentage of the population below the poverty line, and compel them to reside in slum households. The probabilistic models—while formalizing some of these statements—hold that the expected rural-urban income differentials are much larger for the rural poor than for the non-poor, and hence the poor have a higher propensity to migrate to the urban areas (Harris-Todaro, 1970). Todaro (1969) envisaged a two-stage migration process: in the first stage, migrants enter the 'urban traditional' sector (informal sector), due to their limited access to the 'modern sector' (formal sector). In the second stage, with a rise in the duration of their stay, workers in the urban traditional sector are likely to acquire skills and graduate to jobs in the formal sector, or what Todaro called the 'eventual attainment of a more permanent modern sector job'. In most of these studies, the best way of handling urban poverty is seen in terms of the implementation of rural development programmes.

These propositions have, however, been challenged at various levels, as indicated above. Banerjee and Kanbur (1981) argued that those in the middle-income groups have a higher propensity to migrate than those in the bottom or upper-income brackets. To infer that poor villagers are the most likely to migrate from the fact that poor villages expel more migrants is to commit an ecological fallacy (Lipton, 1980). Further, the interpretation of urban poverty in terms of a rural spillover has also been challenged on empirical grounds (Mitra, 1992; and Mills and Mitra, 1997). Papola (1981) and Banerjee (1986) found no evidence to support the assumption that migrants were predominantly located in lower rungs of activities, namely, the informal service sector.

As already emphasized, the work of Banerjee and Bucci (1994) based on the labour market in Delhi evidenced rural-based searches for urban jobs. It confirmed that about one-half of the rural migrants moved after fixing a job or after receiving assurances of employment from those with whom they have had contact in the urban areas. This proportion was almost the same among both formal and informal sector entrants, indicating that informal sector jobs also act as pull factors for migration rather than offering only a stopgap arrangement, as the probabilistic models would hold. On the whole, the contact factor plays a crucial role in obtaining the desired employment within a short span of time.

Further, we argue here that migrants in low-income households prefer to reside near the workplace and that the role of the contact is not confined to merely providing information on jobs. The contact also often provides shelter in the initial stages and helps the entrant to settle down. The co-villagers, relatives, kith and kin, and friends have a strong tendency to live in the vicinity of the early settlers primarily because the jobs obtained through contacts are quite similar to those of the contact persons, particularly in the case of manual and unskilled jobs, as observed by Banerjee (1984).

The urge to reside near the workplace is determined by many factors, some of which could be traced to the very nature of the activities the migrants perform. The self-employed workers in petty manufacturing and repairing activities often have their enterprises within the household premises (see Sethuraman, 1976). Similarly the self-employed and wage labourers in trading activities are required to use their workplace for residential purposes as well, from the point of view of security. Sometimes their encroachment on public land invites the threat of demolition from the municipal authorities, and their constant vigilance of the unit of operation may be essential. At other times they are engaged by their employers outside the working hours to check burglary. This enables them to reduce their expenditure on rent, thus reducing their cost of living in the city. Besides, community latrines and the provision of drinking water in the marketplace induce many of them to reside close to their workplace.

Another reason to stay in the vicinity can be identified in terms of multi-jobs that the members of the low-income migrant households usually take up. Women who combine their household activities with jobs outside the home (for example, domestic maids) are engaged in similar kinds of jobs but in a large number of households, and prefer to have both the place of work and the place of residence in the same vicinity. Even if the total income earned from all jobs is less than the income which could have been earned from the job available at a distant place, the former option would be preferred as long as the cost of commuting and the opportunity cost of the time spent on commuting are larger than the potential earnings at a distant place.

Let Wi be the wage rate earned from activity i and Xi be the time spent on activity i in the neighbourhood. Further, let Wf and Xf represent the wage rate and the time to be spent corresponding to the high-income job at a distant place, Tc the transport cost, and X the time to be spent on commuting. W is taken to be the average of all Wi's, used for computing the opportunity cost of the time spent on travel. Thus, if

$$\Sigma WiXi > WfXf - Tc - WX,$$

it would be an optimal decision to work in the places close to one's residence, forgoing what s(he) could have earned otherwise. Perhaps this could explain what Banerjee (1984) observed in Delhi, that even a majority of the informal wage sector entrants, who are believed to be the vulnerable lot relatively speaking, did not continue their job search after joining the first job.

The desire of the late entrants to reside in the neighbourhood close to their relatives and friends or co-villagers springs from economic factors as well as sociological and political considerations. With wide regional diversities in the cultural backgrounds of the migrants in the face of their difficulties to adapt themselves to an urban cosmopolitan culture of the upper-income groups, their urge to keep alive and enjoy in the city their cultural identity induces them to reside in close proximity to each other. The multilingual and multiethnic identities of the citizens make such a choice even more important. Thus, the more heterogeneous culturally and ethnically an area/country is, the more likely it is that migrants would seek to settle in and around the areas of their brethren. Besides, as mentioned above, the activities of the contact persons (early entrants) and the late entrants being mostly similar, the sharing of family or individual endowments and assets in their pursuit of economic goals is a natural outcome. Collective efforts made by the migrants help delay the slum demolition programmes and secure political patronage.

After discussing the importance of contacts in securing jobs and the desire to reside in groups formed on the basis of caste-kinship-co-villager bonds and the preference of the low-income migrant households to locate near the workplace, we now turn to the development of various nodes (centres) within the city, each characterized by specialized activities. As the literature on agglomeration (particularly the localization) economies suggests, firms conducting similar activities tend to locate close to each other in order to reap the economies of scale (Henderson, 1988). This argument, usually made at the inter-city level to explain the differences in the kinds of activities in which cities specialize, can be extended to the intra-city level, which then helps us see the heterogeneity across space even within a specific city. Hence, different centres within a city would cater to specialized activities, though from the point of view of the overall city all activities would appear to exist within its territory, thus creating the myth of a vast urban labour market. The heterogeneity of the city structure across space has also been documented empirically; the study by Dupont and Mitra (1995) divided the city of Delhi into several small units—census charges—and observed wide interspatial variations of socio-economic characteristics and activities. Further, they also found an incidental matching of these socio-economic variables with the geographic zones of the city.

Keeping in view some of these aspects on the working of networks and the diversified economic structure of the city, we present our analysis of the urban labour market based on the survey results of the slum dwellers. However, before turning to the econometric work, we present some of the descriptive statistics to better understand the urban labour market issues. The next section examines the employment and occupational structure of the slum dwellers and relates them to age, education, caste and earnings. In Section 3.3 a multinomial logit model for occupational choice is estimated in the light of the discussions made in the preceding paragraphs. The importance of networks and the physical segmentation of the urban labour market are some of the major hypotheses in the light of which the model is specified. Section 3.4 estimates an earning function to emphasize the variations across gender, age, caste, and occupation. Finally, Section 3.5 summarizes the major findings.

3.2 Broad Patterns

The questionnaire sought information pertaining to the nature of employment such as self-employment, casual employment, and regular wage salaried employment, and also the exact description of the occupations in which they were engaged. Based on this detailed description about 11 categories of occupations were formed: (i) professionals, (ii) sales workers, (iii) trading, (iv) personal service, (v) manufacturing, (vi) commercial service, (vii) transport, (viii) tailoring, knitting, etc., (ix) construction, (x) security workers, and (xi) repairing workers.[1] Hereafter, these are the broad categories to which we will refer.

It may be noted from Table 3.1 that construction and manufacturing account for more than 30 per cent of the total workers from slum households. Next to these are trade, followed by personal services, sales and commercial services which together account for around 50 per cent of the total workers (Table 3.1). About 40 per cent of the workers are found to be illiterate, and a large majority of them are engaged in construction, personal services, sales, and trade (Table 3.1). Next to the illiterates, the second largest group is formed by those who studied between classes 6 and 9. The occupational

TABLE 3.1: PERCENTAGE DISTRIBUTION OF SLUM WORKERS BY OCCUPATION AND EDUCATIONAL LEVEL

Occupation Groups	Level of Education							Total
	Illiterate	Literate	Studied till Class 3	Class 4 and 5	Class 6 to 9	Secondary	Above Secondary	
Professional	2.8	0.0	6.3	3.4	5.5	8.6	21.3	5.5
Sales	14.5	12.0	10.9	12.9	12.5	9.3	11.2	12.8
Trade	11.7	28.0	14.1	14.3	15.1	16.4	21.3	14.7
Personal Service	19.9	14.0	23.4	10.2	9.6	2.1	4.5	13.4
Manufacturing	8.0	8.0	9.4	15.6	8.1	12.9	4.5	9.3
Commercial Service	9.9	6.0	7.8	9.5	13.3	13.6	12.4	10.9
Transport	2.4	6.0	1.6	2.7	4.1	5.0	2.2	3.2
Tailoring, Knitting, etc.	1.0	6.0	3.1	2.7	3.0	7.9	1.1	2.7
Construction	27.6	12.0	20.3	25.2	20.7	19.3	13.5	22.9
Security	0.0	2.0	0.0	0.7	1.5	0.7	3.4	0.8
Repairing	2.2	6.0	3.1	2.7	6.6	4.3	4.5	3.8
Total	100	100	100	100	100	100	100	100
	(39.5)	(4.00)	(5.11)	(11.7)	(21.5)	(11.1)	(7.1)	

Note: The percentage shares in each of the columns are calculated relative to the column total. Figures in parentheses give the percentage shares of each column total in the total sample (1258).

structure of these workers does not seem to be very different from that of the illiterates except for the fact that commercial services engaged a slightly larger percentage of workers in this group than the illiterate workers. Though only 7 per cent of the workers seem to have acquired an education beyond the secondary level, their occupational pattern appears to be very different from that of the illiterates. Professional, sales, and trade activities account for more than 80 per cent of the workers who attained an education beyond the secondary level.

The age profile of the workers presents no strong evidence in favour of the existence of child labour in the slums (Table 3.2). This could be because of the growing campaign against child labour, which possibly prevented or discouraged a large number of slum households from reporting the overt participation of children in the labour market. In our earlier study also, we noted a similar feature, which then prompted us to devise alternative means to gauge the existence of child labour in the slums (Gupta and Mitra, 1997). A significant number of dropouts from schools, particularly in self-employed households, provides indirect support to our hypothesis that in such households children are largely engaged in income-generating activities either directly or indirectly; they help the adult members of the households in running the enterprise and/or in conducting the household activities.

Nearly 70 per cent of the workers are in the age bracket 21 to 40. It is important to note that the occupational distribution with a rise in age shows a tendency to shift away from activities such as sales, construction, and manufacturing and towards trade, commercial services, and personal services. Less than one-fifth of the workers are women, which is possibly a gross underestimate; since many of them wish to combine household activity with income-yielding activity outside or inside the home, the participation of women in the labour market mostly follows as a residual choice (Table 3.2). While female workers are largely engaged in personal services (around 56 per cent), male workers are mostly absorbed in construction, sales, trade, and commercial services, which together account for around 68 per cent. Chapter 7 examines in detail the issues relating to women employment.

Table 3.3 gives the distribution of non-migrants and migrants by duration of residence across various occupational categories. It is noted that the incidence of all-duration migration in the total number

TABLE 3.2: PERCENTAGE DISTRIBUTION OF SLUM WORKERS BY OCCUPATION AND AGE BRACKETS

Occupation Groups	Age Groups						Total
	Up to 14	15–20	21–30	31–40	41–55	55 and above	
Professional	7.1	7.6	6.7	4.7	3.4	0.0	5.5
Sales	7.1	18.4	16.4	9.0	9.6	7.5	12.8
Trade	0.0	11.3	13.3	14.7	20.2	25.0	14.7
Personal Service	35.7	15.8	10.3	13.2	14.0	30.0	13.4
Manufacturing	35.7	10.8	9.7	8.0	7.9	10.0	9.3
Commercial Service	0.0	6.3	8.3	13.5	15.7	12.5	10.9
Transport	7.1	3.2	3.6	2.8	2.2	5.0	3.2
Tailoring, Knitting, etc.	0.0	2.5	2.9	2.6	3.4	0.0	2.7
Construction	0.0	17.1	24.5	26.0	21.3	10.0	22.9
Security	0.0	0.0	0.5	1.4	1.1	0.0	0.8
Repairing	7.1	7.0	3.8	4.0	1.1	0.0	3.8
Total	100	100	100	100	100	100	100
	(1.1)	(12.6)	(35.4)	(33.6)	(14.1)	(3.2)	

Note: See Table 3.1.

TABLE 3.3: PERCENTAGE DISTRIBUTION OF SLUM WORKERS BY MIGRATION STATUS AND OCCUPATION

Occupation	Migration Status								
	Non-Migrants	Mig. up to 1 year	2–3 years	4–5 years	6–7 years	8–10 years	11–15 years	16–20 years	20 yrs above
Professional	8.1	18.2	3.4	9.8	5.8	4.9	4.9	4.2	2.5
Sales	13.1	0.0	10.3	34.1	11.5	17.6	12.0	11.5	9.4
Trade	9.6	27.3	10.3	12.2	17.3	12.7	19.1	13.0	21.3
Personal Service	16.7	9.1	17.2	7.3	13.5	9.8	10.7	14.9	11.9
Manufacturing	8.7	0.0	13.8	7.3	9.6	9.8	11.6	9.6	7.4
Commercial Service	15.2	9.1	10.3	0.0	7.7	4.9	5.8	12.6	13.4
Transport	4.2	0.0	0.0	2.4	5.8	2.9	3.1	3.1	2.0
Tailoring and Knitting, etc.	0.6	0.0	10.3	2.4	5.8	2.0	3.1	3.8	3.0
Construction	18.2	27.3	24.1	24.4	15.4	29.4	26.7	21.5	26.2
Security	0.3	0.0	0.0	0.0	1.9	2.0	1.3	1.1	0.0
Repairing	5.4	9.1	0.0	0.0	5.8	3.9	1.8	4.6	3.0
Total	100	100	100	100	100	100	100	100	100
	(26.6)	(0.9)	(2.3)	(3.3)	(4.1)	(8.1)	(17.9)	(20.7)	(16.10)

Note: See Table 3.1.

of workers in our sample is more than 70 per cent. Around 55 per cent of the workers are reported to be long-duration migrants (that is, more than 10 years of duration), and short-duration migrants (that is, up to 3 years) comprise only 3 per cent of the workers. Employment in certain activities seems to change significantly with the duration of residence. Manufacturing, for example, does not employ any of those who migrated in last one year or so. Its share shoots up to around 14 per cent among those who migrated in the last 2 to 3 years; thereafter it varies more or less between 7 to 11 per cent. This is indicative of the fact that jobs in activities such as manufacturing are available only when migrants develop access to information after they continue to reside in the urban areas. On the one hand, trading attracts both very short and very long-duration migrants (20 years and above), although due to different reasons. Those who migrated in the last one year or so are employed in this activity, possibly due to the lack of entry barriers and low-skill requirements. On the other hand, those who have worked in this sector for a considerably long period of time have possibly moved up the social ladder by operating and expanding their own enterprises. Hence, in understanding the occupational choice of slum workers the duration of migration needs to be considered as an important variable. It is interesting to note that many of the long-duration migrants have been residing in the city for more than 20 years or so. This is suggestive of strong rural-urban links, which are not merely of a transitory nature. Hence, demolition of slums/or eradication of informal sector activities from the city must not be perceived as a solution to the problems of city growth. This is not because this involves the livelihood of many people but also because several activities which they undertake are conducive to the economic growth of the cities. Mobility that has taken place over the years as a natural response to economic opportunities cannot be scrapped unless development disparities between the place of origin and the place of destination are eliminated.

Distribution of workers by employment categories reveals that more than 40 per cent of them are engaged as casual labour; and the share of self-employment is also quite high (more than 27 per cent). This implies that a large number of slum households are vulnerable to uncertainties of the job market and hence experience fluctuations in income. Those who are self-employed may not directly face labour market uncertainties but in terms of earnings, as we will discuss later in this chapter, they do experience instability due to climatic, seasonal, and other kinds of variations in the demand for their products and services.

The cross-classification of workers by employment categories and occupation groups shows that certain occupations like services (both commercial and personal) are characterized by casual employment. More than 75 per cent of the workers in these occupations are in casual jobs (Table 3.4). Even in manufacturing more than 70 per cent are in casual employment. Occupations such as trading are largely dominated by the self-employed workers. On the other hand, sales involve both casual labour and the self-employed. Even those who are professionals do not seem to have regular jobs. It is only construction which mostly offers regular wage jobs. Jobs offered by contractors for a certain period of time are possibly indicative of this pattern.

For a better understanding of the distribution of slum households across Delhi we divided all the 30 sample clusters into seven zones: (i) south, (ii) central, (iii) north-west, (iv) west, (v) east, (vi) north-

TABLE 3.4: CROSS-CLASSIFICATION OF WORKERS BY OCCUPATION AND EMPLOYMENT CATEGORIES

(*in %*)

Occupation Group	Employment Categories			Total
	Casual Emp.	Regu. Wage/ Salaried Emp.	Self-Emp.	
Professional	92.8	0.0	7.2	100.0
Sales	27.3	31.7	41.0	100.0
Trade	8.1	3.2	88.6	100.0
Personal Service	76.3	5.9	17.8	100.0
Manufacturing	63.2	13.7	23.1	100.0
Commercial Service	94.9	3.6	1.5	100.0
Transport	52.5	12.5	35.0	100.0
Tailoring, Knitting, etc.	17.7	23.5	58.8	100.0
Construction	8.7	90.6	0.7	100.0
Security	90.0	0.0	10.0	100.0
Repairing	45.8	18.8	35.4	100.0
Total	42.8	29.5	27.7	100.0

Note: Percentage distribution is given relative to the row total.

east, and (vii) north. It may be noted from Table 3.5 that different regions specialize in different activities. For example, in the zones of east and north-east Delhi commercial services account for about 23 and 24 per cent of the workers. Manufacturing is significant in north and north-west Delhi. The south zone shows a larger share of personal services than all the other zones. Trade is, of course, almost uniformly spread out in all the zones. The percentage of workers engaged in trade is mostly between 15 and 18 per cent except in the southern and western zones. The share of construction is highest in west Delhi (31 per cent), followed by the central, south, and north-west zones (Table 3.5). These patterns provide us with insights on the basis of which we can model the occupational choice.

3.3 Econometric Modelling of Occupational Choice

In the last section, we noted major variations in occupations across zones, age groups, sexes, levels of education, and migration status. We, therefore, retain these variables in specifying the model for occupational choice. The appropriate specification in this context is the multinomial logit model. As the parameters for all the sub-groups cannot be estimated, the occupation group 9, i.e. OCCP8 has been used as the reference category, that is, parameters for this group have been set to 0.

Other variables introduced in the model are caste, household size, asset, and network. Variables such as age (AGE), household size (HHSZ), and duration of migration (DMIG) are taken in terms of their actual values. The rest of the variables are taken mostly in the form of dummies. GEND is the gender dummy, representing 0 for males and 1 for females. There are 7 zones, for which 6 zone dummies (Zone 1 to Zone 6) have been introduced. CAST takes a value of 1 for scheduled castes and scheduled tribes, and for the rest of the population, 0. The dummy for education (EDUC) makes a distinction between illiterates (0) and literates (1), including those who have attained higher levels of education. The dummy ASSET represents households which have cultivable land and/or house with a value of 1, and for households without these assets, the value is 0.

In accessing jobs, as noted both in our survey as well as in the surveys done by other researchers (Banerjee, 1985), networks are of great importance. These networks operate through various channels

TABLE 3.5: OCCUPATIONAL DISTRIBUTION OF WORKERS IN VARIOUS ZONES

Occupation Groups	Southern	Central	North-West	Western	Eastern	North-East	Northern	Total
Professional	5.9	2.8	4.6	3.7	7.6	6.1	7.3	5.5
Sales	12.1	13.3	15.3	13.1	8.2	12.3	18.8	12.8
Trade	13.2	15.2	16.3	13.1	15.8	18.5	15.6	14.7
Personal Service	22.2	10.5	9.7	10.3	10.7	6.1	6.3	13.4
Manufacturing	5.9	7.6	17.3	6.1	6.6	9.2	20.8	9.3
Commercial Service	8.0	11.4	7.1	8.0	23.0	24.6	2.1	10.9
Transport	2.6	6.7	2.0	2.3	5.1	1.5	3.1	3.2
Tailoring, Knitting, etc.	2.8	1.4	0.0	3.3	4.6	3.1	3.1	2.7
Construction	24.3	24.8	23.0	31.0	16.3	16.9	14.6	22.9
Security	0.8	1.9	0.5	1.4	0.0	0.0	1.0	0.8
Repairing	2.1	3.8	4.1	7.5	2.0	1.5	7.3	3.8
Total	100	100	100	100	100	100	100	100
	(30.8)	(8.3)	(15.5)	(16.9)	(15.6)	(5.2)	(7.6)	

Note: See Table 3.1.

such as relatives, co-villagers, neighbours, friends, members of the same caste groups, and so on. In order to capture the impact of networks in accessing jobs or information pertaining to the job market, we have introduced three dummies. NETWORK1 takes a value of 1 for individuals who got help from relatives (immediate relatives, spouse's relatives, and general relatives) and 0 for the rest; NETWORK2 captures the impact of help received from co-villagers, members of the same caste groups, community fellows, and friends, taking a value of 1 for them and 0 for the rest; NETWORK3 makes a distinction between individuals who received help from employers, NGOs, private companies, and leaders, and the rest, with values of 1 and 0 respectively. Those individuals who did not receive any help from anyone and who mostly depended on their personal efforts to find a job constitute a group which is taken as the reference category in specifying these network dummies.

It may be noted from Table 3.6 that for professionals (OCCP0) both household size and duration of migration have a negative effect. Workers from larger household size (HHSZ) are perhaps less endowed with skills which prevents them from graduating to better jobs. The coefficient of EDUC is positive and highly significant, implying that literates and educated individuals are more likely to get these jobs. Besides, women have a higher probability of getting these jobs. NETWORK1 and NETWORK3, representing the impact of relatives and NGOs, etc., respectively, are highly significant, indicating the existence of both informal and formal flows of information pertaining to the job market. Interestingly, scheduled castes/scheduled tribes are not found to show a higher probability of being located in these jobs. Zones 2, 3, and 4 are less likely to conduct such activities or, in other words, these zones are less likely to have slum dwellers working as professionals.

Among sales workers (OCCP1), CAST shows a negative impact and only NETWORK1 plays a significant role in accessing jobs. Zones 2 and 4 show a lower probability of having sales workers.

Women have a higher probability of joining trading activities (OCCP2). Age plays a negative role, meaning that older workers are less expected to participate in these jobs. CAST again takes a negative coefficient and EDUC turns out to be positive and highly significant. Relatives provide an important support in accessing jobs (NETWORK1), and among various zones, Zone 4 shows a lower probability of locating workers in these activities.

TABLE 3.6: OCCUPATIONAL CHOICE FUNCTION: MULTINOMIAL LOGIT MODEL (ESTIMATE: MLE)

	OCCP0	OCCP1	OCCP2	OCCP3	OCCP4
EDUC1	1.37 (4.02)*	0.05 (0.25)	0.85 (4.00)**	0.62 (2.29)**	0.72 (2.88)*
HHSZ	-0.14(-1.87)	0.08(1.47)	0.07(1.33)	-0.18(-2.67)*	0.02(0.39)
DMIG	-0.13(-2.58)	-0.05(-1.36)***	0.02(0.58)	-0.08(-1.84)**	-0.01(-0.24)
CAST	-.50(-1.76)**	-0.94(-4.41)*	-0.76(-3.74)*	-0.12(-0.46)	-0.37(-1.58)**
GEND	1.34(2.78)*	0.17(0.39)	0.73(1.90)**	4.40(12.77)**	1.40(3.68)*
AGE	0.05(0.28)	-0.01(-0.83)	0.03(2.96)	0.03(2.57)*	0.003(0.23)
ASSET	0.68(1.60)**	0.23(0.79)	0.15(0.55)	0.04(0.13)	-0.13(-0.43)
NETWORK1	1.31(3.59)*	1.19(4.34)	1.32(5.05)*	1.61(4.68)*	1.45(4.60)*
NETWORK2	-1.13(-1.47)***	0.29(0.92)	-0.18(-0.54)	0.89(2.44)*	0.69(1.97)*
NETWORK3	1.20(3.19)	0.04(0.11)	-0.27(-0.76)	0.61(1.59)***	1.26(3.87)*
ZONE1	-0.75(-1.38)***	-0.67(-1.64)***	-0.53(-1.24)	0.89(1.48)***	-1.66(-3.81)*
ZONE2	-2.01(-2.54)*	-0.95(-1.90)**	-0.73(-1.43)***	-0.05(-0.07)	-1.84(-3.32)*
ZONE3	-1.11(-1.81)**	0.59(-1.34)***	-0.45(-1.00)	0.08(0.12)	-0.74(-1.71)***
ZONE4	-1.53(-2.49)*	-1.04(-2.41)*	-0.85(-1.88)**	0.16(0.25)	-1.95(-4.08)*
ZONE5	0.03(0.06)	-88(-1.79)**	-0.16(-0.33)	0.70(1.04)	-1.37(-2.71)*
ZONE6	-0.34(-0.43)	-0.35(-0.58)	0.05(0.09)	-0.001(-0.001)	-1.06(-1.65)***
CONSTANT	-1.25(-1.34)***	0.22(0.34)	-2.02(-3.09)*	-3.20(-3.55)*	-0.64(-0.89)

(contd.)

TABLE 3.6 (contd.)

	OCCP5	OCCP6	OCCP7	OCCP9	OCCP10
EDUC1	0.80(3.25)*	0.65 (1.69)***	1.82 (3.51)*	20.76 (0.004)	1.02 (2.70)*
HHSZ	-0.007(-0.13)	0.14(1.47)***	0.04(0.39)	-0.01(-0.44)	-0.06(-0.70)
DMIG	-0.07(-1.75)***	-0.06(-0.90)	0.13(1.65)***	-0.004(0.03)	-0.02(-0.29)
CAST	0.55(2.19)*	-1.16(-3.14)*	1.24(-3.14)*	-0.16(0.24)	-0.37(-1.12)
GEND	1.70(4.69)*	-0.65(0.62)	1.46(2.34)*	-30.09(0.001)	0.10(0.13)
AGE	0.05(3.93)*	0.004(0.18)	0.001(0.03)	0.06(1.52)***	-0.02(-1.20)
ASSET	-0.23(-0.84)	-0.21(-0.48)	0.07(1.64)***	18.63(0.003)	-0.70(-1.72)***
NETWORK1	1.63(5.28)*	0.90(2.04)*	0.69(1.42)***	1.19(1.29)*	1.87(4.69)*
NETWORK2	0.72(1.90)***	-0.03(-0.05)	-0.32(-0.0001)	1.78(2.28)*	0.22(0.39)*
NETWORK3	1.56(5.06)	0.17(0.32)	-0.29(0.51)	-30.55(0.0001)	0.72(1.38)***
ZONE1	-0.73(0.92)***	-0.43(-0.59)	-0.45(-1.62)	0.85(-0.68)***	-1.73(-2.83)*
ZONE2	-0.82(0.96)*	-0.06(0.08)	-0.17(-1.18)	-0.46(-0.35)	-1.70(-2.31)*
ZONE3	-0.58(0.69)**	-0.87(-1.04)	-32.57(0.0001)	-1.52(-1.02)	-0.18(-1.89)**
ZONE4	-0.60(0.73)*	-1.97(-1.22)	-0.65(-0.84)	-0.78(-0.63)	-1.74(-1.32)
ZONE5	1.89(2.31)*	0.21(0.28)	-0.62(0.79)	-31.53(0.0001)	-1.62(-2.20)*
ZONE6	1.92(2.18)*	-0.88(-0.71)	-0.003(-0.03)	-31.53(-0.0001)	-2.04(-1.76)**
CONSTANT	-4.56 (4.60)*	-2.08(-1.90)**	-4.32(-3.24)*	-43.20(0.0001)*	-0.02(-0.02)

Note: OCCP8 is the comparison group, N=1258. Figures in parentheses are t-ratios. The asterisk marks *, **, and *** represent significance at 5,10, and 20 per cent levels, respectively. The chi-square value is 905.38, which is significant at the 1 per cent level.

It is incorrect to believe that illiterates are more likely to be engaged in personal services (OCCP3). Similarly, it is not correct to suggest that workers from larger households are hard-pressed to find a job and that hence they land up in personal services since entry barriers are mostly absent in these activities. Women, as expected, have a higher probability of being engaged in these jobs. Corresponding to manufacturing (OCCP4), literates relative to illiterates and women workers show a higher probability. All the three network dummies are highly significant. Zones 1, 2, 4, and 5 are less likely to have workers in manufacturing.

In the case of commercial services (OCCP5) EDUC, CAST, GEND, and AGE all have a positive impact. Relatives and NGOs, etc., represented by NETWORK1 and NETWORK3 respectively are highly significant. Zones 5 and 6 seem to have a higher probability of locating these workers. It is interesting to note that jobs in activities such as personal services are usually not available to lower-caste individuals, whereas commercial services are less affected by such factors.

In transport (OCCP6) scheduled castes are less likely to be employed. The role of relatives in getting access to these jobs again turns out to be significant. Tailoring and knitting (OCCP7) have a higher probability of employing women than men. Scheduled castes/ Scheduled tribes are less likely to be engaged in these jobs as well, possibly because of the lack of skill. Literates have an edge over illiterates in joining these occupations.

Security workers (OCCP9) mostly access jobs through friends and co-villagers, and repairing workers (OCCP10) through relatives. Literacy places a higher probability of finding a job in the repairing activities. Zones 1, 2, and 5 are less likely to house the repairing workers.

As already mentioned, the parameters in a multinomial logit model are estimated with reference to parameters of a particular category being set to 0. Hence, interpretation is not invariably unambiguous. Therefore, marginal effects need to be calculated to confirm the interpretation made on the basis of the estimate of the parameters.

The marginal effects reported in Table 3.7 are more or less in conformity with what has been suggested above. For construction activity (OCCP8), for which parameters were set to 0, observations can be made based on the marginal effects. Illiterates seem to have a

TABLE 3.7: MARGINAL EFFECTS: OCCUPATIONAL CHOICE MODEL

Exp. Variables	P0	P1	P2	P3	P4	P5
EDUC	0.035886	-0.0852	0.0197	-0.0128	0.002	0.0090
HHSZ	-0.007237	0.0110	0.0111	-0.0234	0.0029	0.002
DMIG	-0.005652	-0.0027	0.0075	-0.0074	0.0018	-0.0045
CAST	-0.00939	-0.0770	-0.0624	0.0284	-0.0036	0.0962
GEND	0.076909	0.0296	0.1172	0.5982	0.1365	0.1927
AGE	-0.00047	-0.0030	0.0026	0.0028	-0.0010	0.0037
ASSET	0.026218	0.0037	-0.0075	-0.0212	-0.0307	-0.0470
NETWORK1	0.012734	0.0147	0.0367	0.0720	0.0352	0.0605
NETWORK2	-0.026897	0.1178	0.0667	0.2042	0.1230	0.478
NETWORK3	0.054753	-0.0206	-0.0692	0.0547	0.0985	0.1485
ZONE1	-0.026978	-0.0531	-0.0400	0.1538	-0.1303	0.1464
ZONE2	-0.081616	-0.0543	-0.0295	0.0638	-0.1222	0.1464
ZONE3	0.002806	0.0737	0.1042	0.1663	0.0728	0.1898
ZONE4	-0.05571	-0.0670	-0.0482	0.0910	-0.1327	0.1216
ZONE5	0.015582	-0.0805	0.0136	0.1270	-0.1039	0.2325
ZONE6	-0.00241	-0.0064	0.0520	0.0400	-0.4711	0.2420
CONSTANT	0.032736	0.2643	-0.0255	-0.1819	0.1124	-0.2956

(contd.)

TABLE 3.7 (contd.)

Exp. Variables	P6	P7	P8	P9	P10
EDUC	-0.0022	0.0298	-0.1664	0.1603	0.0115
HHSZ	0.0049	0.0012	0.0020	-0.007	-0.0020
DMIG	-0.0009	0.0044	0.0067	0.0003	0.0003
CAST	-0.0265	-0.0246	-0.0762	0.0040	-0.0026
GEND	-0.187	0.0411	0.0147	-2402	0.0062
AGE	-0.0003	-0.0003	-0.0031	0.0004	-0.0013
ASSET	-0.0129	0.0235	-0.0455	-0.1474	-0.0342
NETWORK1	0.0056	-0.0105	-0.2463	0.0009	0.0302
NETWORK2	0.0194	-0.8490	0.1456	0.0193	0.0325
NETWORK3	-0.0008	-0.0024	-0.0453	-0.2460	0.0198
ZONE1	-0.0054	-0.0053	-0.0593	-0.0047	-0.0559
ZONE2	0.0188	-0.0174	0.1240	0.0005	-0.0446
ZONE3	0.0093	0.8480	0.2659	-0.0029	-0.0007
ZONE4	-0.0144	-0.0035	0.1189	-0.0021	-0084
ZONE5	0.0149	0.0234	0.0569	-0.2503	-0.0525
ZONE6	-0.0.186	-0.0073	0.0685	-0.2484	-0.0662
CONSTANT	-0.0075	-0.0670	0.4229	-0.3308	0.0694

Note: P0 to P10 stand for probabilities for each of the occupations OCCP0 to OCCP10.

TABLE 3.8: EMPLOYMENT CHOICE FUNCTION (ESTIMATE: MLE)

Exp. Variables	EMP0	EMP1
EDUC	0.03(0.16)	-0.83 (04.98)*
HHSZ	-009 (-2.41)*	0.05 (-1.23)
DMIG	-0.12 (-4.40)*	-0.04 (-1.43)***
CAST	0.68 (4.37)*	0.33 (2.00)*
GEND	1.53 (6.71)*	-0.37 (-1.35)***
AGE	-0.009 (-0.11)	-0.02 (2.45)*
ASSET	0.34 (1.68)***	0.10 (0.45)
NETWORK1	0.14 (0.77)	-1.18 (-5.74)*
NETWORK2	0.96 (3.71)*	0.25 (0.96)
NETWORK3	1.91 (6.78)*	0.43 (1.40)***
ZONE1	1.63 (4.74)*	0.45 (1.57)***
ZONE2	1.59 (5.90)*	0.53 (1.42)***
ZONE3	1.46 (4.01)*	0.37 (1.20)
ZONE4	1.04 (2.89)*	0.27 (0.91)
ZONE5	1.20 (3.29)*	-0.19 (-0.57)
ZONE6	1.82 (3.98)*	0.05 (0.11)
CONSTANT	-1.13 (-2.19)*	1.48 (3.11)*

Note: EMP2 is the comparison group, N = 1258. Figures in parentheses are t-ratios. The asterisk marks *, **, *** are significant at the 5, 10, and 20 per cent levels, respectively. The chi-square value is 371.76, which is significant at the 1 per cent level.

high probability of joining these occupations. NETWORK2 plays a positive role, whereas help from relatives show a negative marginal effect. There seems to be a higher concentraion of construction workers in Zones 2 and 3.

Apart from the 11 occupational groups, 3 employment categories have also been considered to run the multinomial logit model. The results are reported in Table 3.8. The self-employment (EMP2) category is the comparison group. Corresponding to casual employment (EMP0), a large number of variables are found to be significant. With an increase in household size the probability of joining casual employment falls. Long-duration migrants are less likely to be in casual employment—with an increase in the duration of their stay they manage to acquire more information regarding the job market, and hence move out of the domain of the casual employment category. Scheduled castes show a higher probability of joining the casual employment category as compared to the non-scheduled caste category. Similarly, women workers show a higher probability of taking up these jobs compared to men. Both NETWORK2 and NETWORK3 play a positive role in accessing this category of employment. All the six zone-specific dummies have positive coefficients and these are significant.

In the case of regular wage/salaried employment (EMP1), it is surprising to note that literates have a lower probability of getting such employment. This is possibly because of the fact that these jobs are in the lower spectrum of the income ladder (see next section), and hence literates/educated individuals have a lower preference for these jobs. Women are less likely to get regular-wage employment. The age factor also reduces their probability. Scheduled castes show a greater possibility of getting into regular jobs. NETWORK1 is highly significant but it is negatively related to EMP1. NETWORK3 takes a positive coefficient though it is significant only at the 20 per cent level. Across space Zone 1 and Zone 2 are indicative of a higher probability of holding these salaried or regular-wage jobs.

Having assets in terms of cultivable land and/or one's own house is also an important determinant of occupational/employment choice. For example, in the equations for OCCP0 and OCCP7, ASSET takes a positive coefficient though it is not highly significant. However, people with assets are less likely to join repairing work. In the equation for EMP0 also, it is positive and significant, indicating that with assets people dare to take up employment of the unstable type.

3.4 Earnings

It may be noted from Table 3.9 that earnings per person per month vary considerably across occupations and employment categories. Besides, female-male income differentials are quite significant. The average income of self-employed workers is highest among both males and females. While among male workers earnings from self-employment are only marginally higher than their counterparts in casual jobs, for women workers the differences are quite significant. As women tend to combine household activity with income-yielding activity, self-employed women workers are better off; it is easier for them to cross the border line, which in their case is too narrow. It is interesting to note that in casual jobs the average earnings of women are almost half of their male counterparts. The extent of the difference is minimal only in the case of regular wage/salaried jobs.

Across occupations substantial differences exist. Male workers in

TABLE 3.9: AVERAGE EARNINGS (Rs.) PER MONTH BY OCCUPATION AND EMPLOYMENT TYPE

Occupation	Male	Female	Persons
Professional	2873.8	2250	2801.0
	(1912.9)	(975.04)	(1834.97)
Sales	2110.5	1295	2039.5
	(1233.9)	(842.1)	(1227.2)
Trade	2767	1616.1	2679.1
	(2802.4)	(828.7)	(2718.9)
Personal Service	1955.2	952.7	1178.1
	(2468.7)	(4615.5)	(1297.4)
Manufacturing	2201.8	1745.8	2131
	(1743.5)	(1391.4)	(1696.4)
Commercial Service	3441.3	2862.4	3331.4
	(2160.9)	(1882.0)	(2116.5)
Transport	2653.8	2750	2656.3
	(1087.4)	—	(1073.5)
Tailoring and Knitting, etc.	2472.5	1200	2322.5
	(1302.5)	(697.6)	(1307.0)
Construction	2127.9	1466.2	2088.9
	(774.5)	(467.2)	(775.2)
Security	2254.8	—	2254.8
	(649.5)	—	(649.5)
Repairing	2381.9	2000	2366
	(1306.3)	(1414.2)	(1297.1)
Employment Category			
Casual Employment	2597	1360	2214
	(1545.0)	(1204.5)	(1556.3)
Regular Wage/ Salaried	2164	1357	2090
	(1384.8)	(571.8)	(1350.9)
Self-Employment	2620	1583	2529
	(2372.5)	(796.6)	(2296.9)

Note: Figures in parentheses are standard deviations.

commercial services, professional jobs, trade, and transport are relatively better off. There are enormous differences in female-male earnings corresponding to professionals, sales workers, trade, and personal services. These points are discussed in greater detail in Chapter 7.

Tables 3.10 and 3.11 give the cross-classification of workers across various (monthly) income groups, occupations, and employment categories respectively. Both the tables show that a large percentage of low-paying workers are concentrated in personal services and

TABLE 3.10: PERCENTAGE DISTRIBUTION OF WORKERS BY SIZE CLASSES OF EARNINGS (Rs.) AND OCCUPATION

Occupation Groups	Earnings						
	Up to 300	301–500	501–1,000	1,001–1,500	1,501–2,500	2,501-4,000	4,001 and above
Professional	0.0	0.0	3.1	3.2	6.1	7.8	9.4
Sales	10.0	11.4	12.4	17.0	11.6	12.4	9.4
Trade	0.0	0.0	9.3	13.4	15.1	21.1	17.7
Personal Service	40.0	80.0	42.9	18.2	3.3	2.7	1.0
Manufacturing	20.0	2.9	9.9	10.5	10.6	6.0	6.3
Commercial Service	20.0	2.9	5.0	4.5	7.7	16.1	42.7
Transport	10.0	0.0	0.6	1.2	3.8	6.8	2.1
Tailoring and Knitting, etc.	0.0	2.9	3.1	2.4	2.4	2.8	4.2
Construction	0.0	0.0	10.6	27.1	32.6	19.3	4.2
Security	0.0	0.0	0.6	0.0	1.2	1.4	0.0
Repairing	0.0	0.0	2.5	2.4	5.4	3.6	3.1
Total	100	100	100	100	100	100	100
	(0.79)	(2.78)	(12.8)	(19.6)	(39.1)	(17.2)	(7.6)

Note: See Table 3.1.

TABLE 3.11: PERCENTAGE DISTRIBUTION OF WORKERS BY EARNINGS (Rs.) AND EMPLOYMENT CATEGORIES

Occupation Groups	Earnings							Total
	Up to 300	301–500	501–1,000	1,001–1,500	1,501–2,500	2,501–4,000	4,000 and above	
Casual Employment	70.0	71.4	58.4	38.5	34.8	41.3	62.0	42.8
Regular Wage/Salaried	0.0	1.4	23.6	36.0	37.5	22.9	6.5	29.5
Self-Employment	30.0	17.1	18.0	25.5	27.7	35.8	31.5	27.7
Total	100	100	100	100	100	100	100	100
	(0.8)	(2.9)	(12.9)	(19.7)	(39.1)	(17.3)	(7.3)	

Note: See Table 3.1.

casual employment. With an income of Rs. 1,500 to 4,000, a sizeable proportion of workers are employed in activities such as construction, largely dominated by regular-wage employment (as seen from Table 3.4).

The earnings function that we have estimated is taken to be a

TABLE 3.12: EARNINGS FUNCTION; DEP. VAR: INCOME PER MONTH PER WORKER (ESTIMATE: OLS)

Exp. Variables	(1)	(2)
EDUC	0.03(0.16)	-0.83 (04.98)*
EDUC	173.99 (1.72)***	207.11 (2.00)*
DMIG	-0.09 (-0.005)	-4.50 (-0.26)
CAST	-19.87 (-0.21)	23.38 (0.24)
GEND	-740.86 (-4.85)	-1050.49 (-7.93)*
AGE	97.49 (4.59)*	106.25 (4.90)*
$(AGE)^2$	-1.06 (-3.79)**	-1.14 (-3.98)*
NETWORK1	-12.93 (-0.11)	8.91 (0.07)
NETWORK2	-116.71 (-0.79)	-166.71 (-1.09)
NETWORK3	-69.66 (-0.49)	40.55 (0.27)
ZONE1	-101.74 (-0.54)	-164.61 (-0.85)
ZONE2	31.09 (0.13)	32.97 (0.14)
ZONE3	-20.19 (-0.10)	-58.87 (-0.28)
ZONE4	-45.38 (-0.22)	-85.04 (-0.41)
ZONE5	-144.17 (-0.69)	-1.32 (-0.01)
ZONE6	-133.27 (-0.50)	13.85 (0.05)
EMP0		-13.06 (-0.10)
EMP1		-349.17 (-2.70)*
OCCP0	465.51 (1.51)***	
OCCP1	-288.91 (-1.07)	
OCCP2	198.65 (0.75)	
OCCP3	-631.38 (-2.17)*	
OCCP4	-174.55 (-0.62)	
OCCP5	983.93 (3.51)*	
OCCP6	259.31 (0.74)	
OCCP7	-130.04 (-0.35)	
OCCP8	-343.01 (-1.33)***	
OCCP9	-386.48 (-0.68)	
CONSTANT	517.63 (1.10)	398.41(0.93)
Adj.R^2	0.14	0.09
F	9.22	8.35
N	1258	1258

Note: Figures in parentheses are t-ratios. The asterisk marks *, ** and ***are significant at the 5, 10, and 20 per cent levels, respectively.

function of age, (age)^2, education, caste, networks, zones, duration of migration, and occupational classes (alternatively employment categories). The results are reported in Table 3.12. EDUC1 is positively significant, and so also EDUC2 which is taken as an alternative formulation to make a distinction between the senior secondary level and above *vis-à-vis* the rest (result not reported here). Both age and (age)^2 have positive and negative signs respectively, implying that earnings increase with age only till a threshold level. Network dummies, unlike in the equation for occupational choice, do not turn out to be significant in the earnings function. Based on the regression exercise, it is again confirmed that women receive a lower wage as compared to males. Surprisingly, not all the dummies representing various occupations turn out to be significant. Only OCCP3 (personal services) and OCCP5 (commercial services) have negative and positive signs respectively, which are statistically significant. The other two dummies corresponding to OCCP0 and OCCP8 are also significant, though at the 20 per cent level only. While the former raises the income per worker, the latter tends to reduce it. These findings are more or less in conformity with what emerged from the tabular analysis. Scheduled castes/tribes do not seem to be better or worse off relative to the rest.

Instead of occupation categories, if we take the employment categories in the form of dummies in the equation for earnings, EMP1, which represents regular wage/salaried employment, takes a negative coefficient. This is quite surprising because regular employment is expected to yield higher earnings. But the other side of the story is that regular employment offers lower wages, whereas employment with uncertainties yields higher earnings. The average figures corresponding to earnings in different employment categories as given in Table 3.11 conform to this pattern.

3.5 Conclusion

In this chapter we have focused on questions relating to occupational choice, networks, and the physical segmentation of the urban labour market. Both the tabular and econometric analyses are indicative of associations among occupation groups (employment categories) and several individual attributes such as education, migration status, assets, networks, and the preference to reside near the workplace. Certain occupations (or employment categories) are typically characterized by the presence of certain groups of individuals, indicating the significance of factors such as gender and/or caste in the urban labour market. Two important findings relate to the significance of network dummies and the zone-specific dummies in the equations for occupational choice.

The interconnections between network (and the nature of the network) and occupation type are noteworthy. While certain occupations are accessed through relatives (NETWORK1) certain others are acquired through co-villagers, friends, etc. (NETWORK2) and certain others are secured through more formal contacts such as NGOs etc. (NETWORK3), though more than one network in certain occupations do operate simultaneously. On the whole, occupation and network are all in relationship governed by factors such as caste, gender, migration status, and education; these factors determine the the nature of contact and the access to information pertaining to the job market. However, in our analysis the networks are taken as exogenous. Although the informal networks play a major role in securing employment in the urban informal sector, the intricacies and the subtle forms of mechanism that operate in the urban labour market are of significant interest. Without an understanding of these existing modes of operation policy suggestions for the betterment of the urban poor would be incomplete, and may also prove to be misleading.

The contours of associations, however, need to be understood in the perspective of the diverse nature of activities across space, reflecting the heterogeneity of the socio-economic structure of the city. In other words, interconnections between individual endowment of skills and talents, preference for occupation type, and its ultimate selection are reflected in the intra-city variation pattern of city growth in terms of population concentration, dwelling structures and congestion, given the spatial variation in the nature of economic activities within the city. Our second finding relating to the zone-specific dummies is suggestive of such tendencies. That workers only in certain activities are located in certain areas and not in all is indicative of strong differences in the city's socio-economic structure across space, broad overlaps between the place of work and the place of residence of these low-income households, and thus the physical segmentation of the urban labour market. These patterns emphasize that not all slums are of the same type and that hence the problems that slum dwellers face could be quite diverse in nature.

NOTE

1. The detailed lists of occupations have been consolidated to construct the following groups:

 (a) *Professional, etc.*: accountant, bank service, computer operator and other computer related work, doctor, government job, professional tutor, official work, quality controller, worker in an NGO, engaged in fieldwork.

 (b) *Sales*: incense stick seller, agent, assistant shopkeeper, assistant in shop, seller of food products, egg seller, electric shop holder, fish seller, fruit seller, helper, juice seller, waste collector (in local language *kabariwala*), newspaper hawker, salesman, toy seller, balloon seller, liquor seller, vegetable seller, other hawker/vendor.

 (c) *Trade*: exporter, fair attendant, butcher, sweetmeat seller, worker in hotel, tent fixer, worker in medical shop, milk man, petty trader, shopkeeper, servant in woodshop, supplier, teashop owner/worker, worker in timber stall, worker in shop, worker in fish shop, worker with tent contractor, dairy owner, contractor.

 (d) *Personal Service*: barber, cobbler, cook, coolie, dhobi, domestic labour, domestic servant, gardener, health *sevika*, hospital maid, ironing clothes, etc., priest, rotimaker, *sevika*, shoeshiner, clothes washer.

 (e) *Manufacturing*: bag maker, bidi maker, box maker, butcher, screen (in local language *chik*) maker, confectioner, cover maker, dial maker, die fitter, drum maker, factory worker, glass cutter, glass worker, headlight maker, key maker, machine operator, electrical parts maker of, shoe maker, metal processors, medicine maker, printer, printing press operator, scent maker, servant in a flour mill, skilled labour, toffee manufacturer, traditional artisan, worker in workshop.

 (f) *Commercial Service*: airport loader, band player, cable operator, caterer, class IV employees, commentator, helper in Delhi Jal Board, drumplayer (in local language *Dholokwala*), MCD worker, musician, packaging employee, peon, postman, worker in office, sweeper, ward boy.

 (g) *Transport*: auto driver, conductor, driver, rickshaw-puller, tempo driver.

 (h) Tailoring, knitting, etc.

 (i) *Construction*: construction labour, carpenter, mason, marble cutter, painter, plumber, sanitary worker, hand-pump worker, white washing.

 (j) *Security*: constable, home guard, security agency, security guard, watchman.

 (k) *Repairing*: cooker repairing, cycle repairing, diesel mechanic, electrician, refrigerator repairing, gas and cooker repairing, mechanic, motor mechanic, vehicle repairing, sofa repairing, TV mechanic, welder, worker in car shop.

CHAPTER 4

LABOUR MARKET MOBILITY

4.1 Introduction

The 'over-urbanization' thesis argues that migrants move into urban areas as they are pushed out of the agriculture sector. And in the face of limited employment opportunities in the high-productivity sector in the urban areas, they continue to work in the low-productivity urban informal sector. Urban poverty in this sense is nothing but a reflection of rural poverty. But the question which remains unanswered in this context is: why do migrants not return to their homes in the rural areas if they continue to be confined to low-productivity activities in the cities? The answer to this question can be found in the work of the critics of the over-urbanization thesis. The decision to migrate is based on rational grounds; migrants continue to reside in the urban areas even when they do not manage to acquire a formal-sector job precisely because even within the informal sector they manage to experience upward income mobility. They are able to reduce the intensity of poverty which they experience, if not escape it altogether. This argument prompts us to pose a number of questions from the empirical standpoint. Based on the data on slum dwellers we examine in this chapter if workers managed to experience a change in their occupation over time. Even when the broad occupation category remains the same, does the nature of employment change and do income levels rise? If so, what role does the network play in helping them gain access to better-paying jobs? Besides, as slum dwellers continue to stay in the city does the nature of their contact change over time? From this point of view it would be interesting to compare the contacts that helped the later entrants gain access to the present jobs with the contacts that got them their jobs in the past. These are some of the issues which not only interest researchers but also policy makers. If informal mechanisms can enhance the social welfare of the workers then intervention on the part of the government may actually worsen their living conditions instead of bringing about any improvement. Besides, government intervention means placing a burden on the public exchequer which, in other words, is an additional cost to the society. Hence, less beneficial outcomes associated with higher social costs are less preferable to the informal self-efforts of individuals, unless these self-efforts involve considerable negative externalities in terms of health hazards, environmental pollution, or any other such adverse repercussion on the economy.

The organization of this chapter is as follows. In the next section we focus on occupational mobility; Section 4.3 examines the changes in the nature of contacts in accessing jobs. Income mobility is examined in Section 4.4. Section 4.5 summarizes the major findings.

4.2 Occupational Mobility

The ILO report on Kenya (1972) argues that not only the high-wage formal-sector job but also the income opportunity in the informal sector attracts the potential migrant. 'Informal sector employment is undesirable when viewed from above by the formal sector wage or salary earner, but desirable and an independent source of attraction when viewed from below by the rural immigrant' (ILO, 1972, p. 224). The Todaro model (1969) argues that subsequent to their migration to the urban areas the workers search for better opportunities and in due course graduate to employment in the formal sector. Breman (1976), however, argues that the idea of moving to better-paid jobs is mostly fictional because those who join the lower ranks of the urban labour system usually remain there. Standing (1977) also feels that it is difficult for them to escape once they join this sector. 'The ability to perform regular sustained work tends to evaporate through lack of use, and the poor diet and medical treatment available to those in the irregular sector tend to undermine their physical and mental capacity to do sustained work' (Standing, 1977, p. 41). However, within the informal sector the possibility of movement from low-productivity jobs to better-paid jobs does exist, as several studies based on survey data point out.

The informal sector is not necessarily confined exclusively to of low-productivity jobs. As the literature on the relationship between the formal and informal sectors points out, the process of interaction between these two sectors is quite complex. Papola (1981) argues that the size of the informal sector is large in situations of both limited industrial spread and rapid industrialization. In the former case, it is mainly a manifestation of residual absorption of labour, whereas in the latter case both are complementary to each other. Also, in this situation the informal sector is described as being no more a low-productivity sector by virtue of its close linkage with the industrial sector and the income percolating from this sector to the rest of the economy.

As regards the facets of the interaction between the informal sector, on the one hand, and industrialization, on the other, links may be taken to exist through the following channels: (a) labour market, (b) commodity market, and (c) production process. On *a priori* grounds the nature of the relationship between the share of informal sector employment and industrialization can be positive as well as inverse. If informal sector employment is taken to be the outcome of sluggish employment growth in the industry, then it would have a negative relationship with respect to the latter. Tokman (1989) argues that the informal sector shows an 'autonomous element', i.e. activities being not associated with those carried out in the rest of the economy, and is also at the same time closely integrated with the rest of the economy. Further, in a recent paper (Tokman, 1989) he highlights the linkage between poverty and informal-sector employment. While arguing that the chances of reducing the number of informal sector workers by absorbing them into modern activities are slim, he postulates a negative relationship between the high-productivity modern sector employment and the low-productivity informal sector employment. Also, in the study by Hemmer and Mannel (1989) the possibility of an inverse relationship between industrial and informal sector employment exists. With an extension of the formal sector, they argue, demand for labour within this sector at a given minimum wage may increase (or decrease) depending upon the technological conditions which, in turn, at a given volume of labour supply, including the migrants, reduces (or raises) the volume of labour in the informal sector. Stark (1982) argues that with the expansion of the modern sector, new employment opportunities are created which may eliminate some of the informal sector jobs if the activities are competitive. On the other hand, the relationship can be complementary if the expansion of output and employment in the modern sector generates employment in the informal sector through inter-sectoral linkages. When both the forces are at work the net relationship may turn out to be competitive or complementary depending upon the relative strength of the forces. However, in Stark's

(1982) model, as Datta-Chaudhury (1989) argued, the expansion or contraction of the informal sector is basically determined by the growth of the formal sector. On the other hand, Datta-Chaudhury (1989) notes that the informal sector can expand when the formal sector is stagnating or contracting.[1]

Following Papola (1981), we note that the informal sector grows in both the situations of rapid industrialization and sluggish industrial growth. But employment in the informal sector, while it is induced by industrial growth, offers better-paid jobs and hence facilitates rapid upward mobility. Delhi, though not an industrial city, has experienced rapid growth of several other formal sector activities. Many of the informal sector activities have possibly grown in response to the growth of these activities though an equally large proportion of activities might have come up due to population pressure. It would therefore be interesting to examine whether slum dwellers in our sample have been able to locate themselves in better-paid jobs in due course after migrating to the city. A comparison of their first job in the city with their present job can throw light on this question. The Todaro (1969) model suggests that immediately after migrating to the city the rural migrants locate themselves in the informal sector but over time there takes place what he calls the eventual attainment of the modern sector employment. Our hypothesis is that such sectoral movements are not always possible due to the sluggish employment growth in the high-productivity sector; and hence within the informal sector the job search continues and workers shift from low to high-income jobs.

Those who gave a positive response to the question about their past employment have been categorized as per their present and past employment categories in Table 4.1, and as per their present and past occupation categories in Table 4.2.

It is interesting to note from Table 4.1 that among those who are presently engaged in regular-wage/salaried employment, around 51 per cent moved from casual-wage employment. Another 25 per cent stated that they have been in self-employment and only 24 per cent said that they continued to be in regular-wage/salaried employment both in the past and the present.

Among those who are presently in casual jobs, a large majority (62 per cent) were in the same employment category in the past as well. However, around 20 per cent of the present casual workers seem to have lost their regular-wage employment which they had

TABLE 4.1: PERCENTAGE DISTRIBUTION OF WORKERS BY PRESENT AND PAST EMPLOYMENT CATEGORIES

Present Emp. Category	Past Emloyment Category			Total
	Salaried	Casual	Self-Emp.	
Regular-Wage/Salaried	23.9	51.1	25.0	100.0
Casual	20.0	61.8	18.2	100.0
Self-Employed	19.1	50.9	30.0	100.0

Note: The percentages are given relative to the row total.

held in the past. Similarly, around 19 per cent of the self-employed (presently) were working previously as regular-wage earners. Among those who are presently in self-employment, about 51 per cent shifted from casual employment, and another 30 per cent were engaged in the same employment category in the past.

On the whole, there seems to have been some upward shift in terms of the employment category if regular-wage/salaried jobs are taken as the top ranking. As we have noted in the last chapter, the average earnings accruing to workers in regular-wage/salaried jobs are not necessarily higher than those prevailing among workers in casual jobs or self-employment. However, jobs with a steady and assured flow of income may be preferable to those with a fluctuating income, though in terms of averages the latter may yield higher pay-offs. The proportion of those who were in salaried jobs but who are presently in either casual jobs or are in the self-employment category is 45.7 per cent. However, judged on the basis of employment categories the extent of upward movement seems to exceed the downward movement. Besides, of those who remained unemployed or outside the labour market in the past, nearly 45 per cent are found to be engaged in regular-wage/salaried jobs at present.

Some of the activities/occupations in which at least 20 per cent of the workers seem to have been engaged both at present and in the past are professional (23.1 per cent), personal service (22.2 per cent), manufacturing (25 per cent), transport (20 per cent), tailoring, etc. (33.3 per cent), and construction (41.5 per cent). Considerable changes in occupations seem to have taken place though it is quite difficult at this stage to discern the changes that are favourable in terms of occupational mobility. A large number of construction workers seem to have shifted to sales and to trade, accounting for about 32 per cent of

TABLE 4.2: CROSS-CLASSIFICATION OF WORKERS BY PRESENT AND PAST OCCUPATIONS

(*in* %)

Present Occupation	Past Occupation					
	Professional	Sales	Trade	Personal Service	Manufacturing	Commercial Service
Professional	23.1	7.7	7.7	0.0	7.7	7.7
Sale	2.6	10.5	18.4	2.6	5.3	13.2
Trade	4.2	9.9	8.4	2.8	15.5	2.8
Personal Service	11.2	11.1	0.0	22.2	22.2	22.2
Manufacturing	0.0	20.8	8.3	4.2	25.0	00
Commercial Service	3.6	10.7	3.6	10.7	9.6	17.9
Transport	0.0	13.3	6.7	6.7	6.7	0.0
Tailoring, Knitting, etc.	0.0	0.0	33.3	0	0	0
Construction	0.0	7.3	7.3	4.9	14.6	12.2
Security	0.0	25.0	0	0	0	25.0
Repairing	0.0	0	9.1	9.1	9.1	9.1
Total	3.5	10.5	8.9	5.1	12.1	8.6

(contd.)

TABLE 4.2 (contd.)

Present Occupatoin	Past Occupation					
	Transport	Tailoring, Knitting, etc.	Construction	Security	Repairing	Total
Professional	0.0	0.0	30.8	0.0	15.4	100
Sale	10.5	0.0	31.6	2.6	2.6	100
Trade	12.7	4.2	32.4	2.8	4.2	100
Personal Service	0.0	0.0	11.1	0.0	0.0	100
Manufacturing	8.3	0.0	29.2	0.0	4.2	100
Commercial Service	3.6	3.6	35.7	3.6	3.6	100
Transport	20.0	0.0	13.3	6.7	26.7	100
Tailoring, Knitting, etc.	33.3	33.3	0.0	0.0	0.0	100
Construction	2.4	0.0	41.5	2.4	7.3	100
Security	0	0.0	50.0	0.0	0.0	100
Repairing	9.1	9.1	27.3	9.1	9.1	100
Total	8.6	2.3	31.5	2.7	6.2	100

Note: The percentage distribution is given relative to the row total.

the workers in each of these occupations. Around 18 per cent of the total trade workers actually moved from manufacturing and transport. Similarly, around 27 per cent of the construction workers were earlier employed in manufacturing and commercial services.

4.3 Change in Contacts

In accessing present occupations contacts seem to have played a major role (Table 4.3). Around 37 per cent of the currently working individuals stated that they did not take any help from others, and another 8 per cent did not give any specific information regarding the nature of their contacts. The remaining 55 per cent, however, sought help from others in finding a job in the urban labour market. Though the nature of the contacts varies across occupations certain broad patterns are quite evident. Among professionals, the immediate relatives and the present employer turn out to be important contacts. Among sales workers, the same contacts again appear to be dominant though general relatives and co-villagers both account for around 15 per cent of the total. Among trade workers, next to the immediate relatives were the general relatives; in personal services, the inhabitants of the same cluster happened to be the most important source of contacts. Among manufacturing workers also, next to the immediate relatives and employers were the inhabitants of the same cluster who helped find jobs. NGOs played an important role in obtaining jobs in commercial services. Co-villagers and people from the same cluster are two important sources of contacts next to the immediate relatives and the employers who found them the present source of livelihood in construction. On the whole, other than self-help, the immediate relatives and the present employers played an important role in providing employment opportunities and/or changing occupations, and secondly, co-villagers, people from the same neighbourhood, (cluster) and general relatives also assisted in accessing information pertaining to the job market. Private contractors and community leaders do not seem to have offered any significant help in this respect. Even NGOs, except in the case of commercial services, do not seem to have played any major role.

Our next concern is to examine if the same pattern of contacts prevailed in the past as well. (Table 4.4 presents the cross-classification of workers across past occupations and contacts, which they used to obtain jobs.) Apart from the immediate relatives no other source of contacts appears to be of any significance in the past.

TABLE 4.3: PRESENT OCCUPATION AND CONTACTS

Present Occupation	Contacts						
	Imm. Rel.	Spouse's Rel.	General Rel.	Co-villagers	Member of the same caste group	Member of the same cluster	Friends
Professional	18.8	0.0	13.0	1.4	0.0	1.4	0.0
Sale	22.4	0.6	7.5	7.5	1.9	5.0	0.0
Trade	23.2	1.6	7.6	4.9	0.5	3.2	0.0
Personal Service	14.2	3.0	5.3	1.8	2.4	15.4	0.6
Manufacturing	17.9	4.3	5.1	43.4	2.6	10.3	0.0
Commercial Service	17.5	5.8	5.1	2.2	1.5	5.8	0.7
Transport	20.0	2.5	5.0	7.5	2.5	0.0	0.0
Tailoring, Knitting, etc.	23.5	0.0	0.0	0.0	0.0	0.0	0.0
Construction	6.6	2.1	3.1	5.2	1.7	6.3	0.0
Security	20.0	0.0	0.0	20.0	0.0	20.0	0.0
Repairing	33.3	0.0	10.4	4.2	2.1	2.1	2.1
Total	17.0	2.2	5.8	4.3	1.6	6.5	0.2

(contd.)

TABLE 4.3 (contd.)

Present Occupation	Contacts						
	Employer	NGO	Private contractor	Leader	Self	Other	Contact not mentioned
Professional	23.2	1.4	0.0	0.0	34.8	0.0	5.8
Sale	8.7	0.0	0.6	0.0	37.3	1.2	7.4
Trade	4.9	0.5	0.5	1.1	43.8	3.8	4.3
Personal Service	12.4	0.6	0.0	0.0	30.8	21.2	12.4
Manufacturing	18.8	0.0	3.4	0.0	29.9	1.7	2.6
Commercial Service	14.6	10.9	1.5	0.0	19.7	7.3	7.3
Transport	7.5	2.5	2.5	0.0	32.5	2.5	15.0
Tailoring, Knitting, etc.	8.8	2.9	0.0	2.9	50.0	2.9	8.8
Construction	9.4	0.4	1.4	0.7	51.7	1.0	10.4
Security	0.0	0.0	0.0	0.0	30.0	0.0	10.0
Repairing	12.5	0.0	0.0	0.0	18.8	0.0	14.6
Total	11.2	1.7	1.0	0.4	37.4	2.2	8.4

Note: The percentage distribution is given relative to the row total.

TABLE 4.4: PAST OCCUPATION AND CONTACTS

Past Occupation	% of Households who received	
	Help from Immediate Relatives	Self-help
Professional	11.1	66.7
Sales	25.9	18.5
Trade	30.4	30.4
Personal Service	30.8	30.8
Manufacturing	19.4	41.9
Commercial Service	40.9	13.6
Transport	22.7	54.5
Tailoring, Knitting, etc.	16.7	50.0
Construction	25.9	42.0
Security	14.3	28.6
Repairing	6.3	18.8
Total	24.5	35.8

In fact, in some of the occupations such as sales and commercial services the immediate relatives helped to a much greater extent than self-help. Even in trade and personal services both the immediate relatives and self-help benefited almost an equal percentage of workers. The major difference between the present and the past contacts is that self-help in accessing the present jobs turns out to be the most important component in almost all the activities, whereas in the past, the immediate relatives had been either more effective or as effective as self-help in getting jobs in a number of activities.

It may be interesting to assess if there is any close association between the nature of contacts used by individuals to obtain their present occupations and the nature of the contacts used in the past. Among those who utilized the help of the immediate relatives in the past only 27 per cent seem to have continued with the same source of contacts. The rest developed other contacts; almost one-third of them depended on self-effort to venture further into the labour market and possibly to improve their earnings. On the other hand, those who depended on self-effort in the past continued to do so later on as well; about 60 per cent of them accessed their present jobs through self-effort and the rest diversified their contacts. It may be inferred from this that initially with respect to certain activities the immediate relatives by and large matter in seeking an entry into the labour market but at a later stage self-efforts and/ or other sources of contact are crucial for the realization of upward occupational mobility.

4.4 Income Mobility

Finally, we compare the past income and the present income of the workers. Workers have been cross-classified by various size classes formed on the basis of present and past income. Figures along the leading diagonal give the proportion of workers whose income remained in that size class both in the past and the present. In other words, these are the workers who did not experience any significant change in their income in either direction and hence did not move out of these size classes.

The entries above the leading diagonal show the percentage of workers whose income in the past was in higher-size classes as compared to the present. As noted from Table 4.5, most of the entries above the leading diagonal are either 0 or nominal. On the other hand, elements below the leading diagonal showing upward movement in terms of income-size classes are large and account for the bulk of the workers for whom present and past incomes are reported. Some of the entries in particular show significant changes in the income of the workers. Around 47 per cent of those who were in the income-size classes Rs. 0–300, Rs. 301–500, Rs. 501–1,000, and 1,001–1,500 moved to the present income-size class of Rs. 1,501–2,500 and another 23 per cent moved to Rs. 2,501–4,000. Though there is evidence in favour of upward income mobility, cases suggesting downward mobility are also present, i.e. around 83 per cent of those who earned an income of Rs. 2,501 to Rs. 4,000 per month in the past moved to lower-income categories in the present. Similarly, all those from the past income categories of Rs. 4,000 and above slipped to lower-income groups in the present. However, the percentage of those experiencing downward mobility over time is much less than those who could undergo an increase. Nevertheless, the scope for upward mobility seems to exist among those in the lower-income brackets, suggesting the vulnerability of the high-income groups to risks and uncertainties.

As we piece together information on past and present occupation employment categories, contacts, and incomes of the slum workers, there seems to be a substantive improvement in their status over time. Though from the detailed listing of occupations only a marginal number of workers appears to be employed in the formal sector, within the informal sector itself significant upward mobility has taken place. Improvements are to be judged only in terms of change in occupation categories, which we have formed broadly on the basis of

TABLE 4.5: CROSS-CLASSIFICATION OF WORKERS BY PAST AND PRESENT INCOME

Present	Past Income								Total
	0–300	301–500	501–1,000	1,001–1,500	1,501–2,500	2,501–4,000	4,001–5,000	5,000 and above	
0–300	3.7	0.0	1.2	0.0	0.0	0.0	0.0	0.0	1.2
301–500	3.7	0 .0	0.0	0.0	0.0	0.0	0.0	0.0	0.8
501–1,000	5.6	2.0	4.7	2.9	4.5	33.3	0.0	0.0	4.7
1,001–1,500	11.1	11.8	17.6	14.7	9.1	33.3	100	0.0	14.5
1,501–2,500	35.2	56.9	44.7	58.8	50.0	16.6	0.0	100	47.1
2,501–4,000	31.5	19.6	23.5	14.7	22.7	0	0.0	0.0	22.4
4,001–5,000	9.3	2.0	3.5	5.9	9.1	0	0.0	0.0	5.1
5,000 and above	0.0	7.8	4.7	2.9	4.5	16.6	0.0	0.0	4.3
Total	100	100	100	100	100	100	100	100	100
	(21.2)	(20.0)	(33.3)	(13.3)	(8.6)	(2.4)	(10.4)	(0.8)	

Notes: (1) Each column adds up to 100 per cent.
(2) Figures in parentheses across the row add up to 100 per cent.

the detailed listing; intra-occupational upward mobility in terms of income cannot be ruled out. From this it may be inferred that the decision to migrate is not irrational even when the migrant workers are seen to be working within the informal sector for their entire life, providing little support to the graduation hypothesis of the Todaro model (1969). In the absence of occupational diversification in the rural areas, even petty informal sector activities provide a source of livelihood and open up the way for substantial changes to take place in the future as the migrants combine self-efforts with their other sources of contacts. Escaping poverty, therefore, is an outcome of various informal mechanisms that operate simultaneously within the informal sector, engaging workers largely from slum households.

4.5 Conclusion

In this chapter we examined mainly the upward income mobility hypothesis. Though most of the workers seem to be employed in the informal sector both in the past and the present, many of them have experienced significant improvements in terms of earnings. Both inter- and intra-occupational changes within the informal sector itself have been beneficial to the workers. At the entry point into the urban labour market, networks through relatives, and friends are important but at a later stage self-efforts help the workers improve the nature of their jobs and climb up the income ladder. On the whole, though the graduation hypothesis, i.e. transfer of labour from the informal to the formal sector, does not seem to receive much empirical support, movements within the informal sector are substantive and prove to be beneficial. It is evident that at the initial stages networks are of great importance for entering the urban labour market, though it is possible to achieve upward income mobility at the later stages largely through individual effort and self-help.

NOTE

1. Mitra (1994) notes that in relative terms the industrial sector and the informal sector are inversely related, though the elasticity of employment in the informal sector with respect to employment in the industrial sector is positive.

CHAPTER 5

LIVING STANDARDS IN DELHI SLUMS

5.1 Introduction

Most studies on urban slums and poverty tend to regard these as synonymous; policy makers also make little distinction between the two. From the analytical and empirical points of view, however, one may identify at least three different categories of slums. First, indivisibilities of investments and infrastructural facilities create agglomeration economies, which lead to the concentration of population and congestion, eventually resulting in the deterioration of the quality of life in the face of escalating land prices. In such a situation it is not necessarily only the poor households which reside in slums. Second, the preference patterns of certain individuals, as manifested in their consumption patterns, may reveal that housing is given only secondary importance. Individuals avail of poor-quality housing at low prices in order to use their limited savings to purchase consumer durables and to meet other urgent needs and responsibilities. Third, a residual absorption of labour in low-productivity informal sector activities generates meagre earnings, which in the face of the high cost of living in the urban areas force them to reside in slums. It is only this third category of slum households, which overlaps with poor households, and the rest are indicative of very different policy implications (for details see Mitra, 1994). It is, therefore, essential to understand the differences in the processes of slum growth not only from the policy point of view but this is also necessary for a clear understanding of the social and economic forces that determine the standard of living.

The existence of inequality within the slums, as discussed in the next section of this chapter, substantiates the argument of heterogeneity in the behaviour of the slum dwellers. Social factors such as networks and economic considerations influence the decision to migrate, the access of migrants to information pertaining to the job market and their quality of life in the urban areas. Previous studies (Banerjee, 1981, 1985, 1991; Kanappan, 1983) have focused on some of these issues, namely, the information flow along the lines of caste-kinship bonds and through contacts with co-villagers. Stark (1995) also highlights the ways in which the preferences and actions of one family member impinge upon and modify the choice set, the behaviour, and the well-being of other family members. Howevers, more study is needed for an in-depth understanding of the interplay of various factors that make a migrant a likely candidate for upward mobility.

Another major lacuna in poverty studies in India is that most focus on rural poverty, as in absolute terms the rural poor outnumber the urban poor. However, the percentage of the population below the poverty line in the urban areas has not been less significant. The incidence of urban poverty was as high as 45 per cent in 1977–8, which dropped to 38 per cent in 1987–8, and to 32 per cent in 1993–4. Thereafter, as the thin sample results of the NSSO surveys tend to suggest, the head count ratio is indicative of a slightly increasing tendency—at least no major decline seems to have occurred, though in 1999–2000 it was 23.6 per cent. Unfortunately, policy planners and researchers have often interpreted urban poverty purely as a spillover effect of rural poverty, and hence the successful implementation of the rural employment programmes is believed to reduce urban poverty extensively (see Mitra, 1989, 1992).

In the literature on development economics attempts have been made to explain rapid city growth and urbanization—more importantly the ills of urbanization, namely, slums and urban poverty—on the basis of two major hypotheses: (i) unusually rapid rates of population growth which exerted pressure on limited farm acreage and thus pushed landless labour into the cities, and (ii) migrants being pulled into the cities by economic forces such as the squeezing of agriculture by the domestic terms of trade, the diffusion of technology from the developed world favour modern large-scale urban industries, foreign capital flows into the urban infrastructure, housing, power, transportation, and large-scale manufacturing (see Williamson, 1988). Most demographers, favour the first hypothesis as do Lewis's (1954) labour surplus model and Todaro's (1969) probabilistic model. The main cause of rapid urban growth according to the 'over-urbanization thesis', as the literature has popularly termed it, can be traced to the increasing pressure of population on farmland in densely populated agrarian economies. Deficiency of reproducible tangible capital (relative to labour) in the face of high population density exacerbates the problem of rural unemployment and underemployment, which in turn fosters the rural-urban population movement. In the face of limited demand for labour in the formal sector, in particular the organized industrial sector, excess supplies in the urban labour market force the workers and/or migrants to engage in the informal service sector. The low rate of growth of industrial employment and the high rate of rural-to-urban migration make for excessive, even explosive urbanization, involving a transition from rural unemployment to excessive urban underemployment and poverty, which is manifested in the form of vast stretches of slums in the midst of large cities.

This view has, however, been challenged by several scholars primarily because it runs the 'risk of sweeping the urban ills under the rural carpet' (Kannapan, 1983); if migration implies merely the physical transfer of the rural poor to urban areas then urban underemployment and poverty should be short-lived as the decision to migrate to urban areas is based on sound and rational considerations. Besides, the empirical literature offers considerable evidence against the notion that migration is a transitory phenomenon; migrants continue to reside in cities as they enjoy a better standard of living compared to their living standards prior to their out-migration. Banerjee and Kanbur (1981) argue that those in the middle-income groups have a higher propensity to migrate than those in the bottom- or upper-income brackets. Further, the interpretation of urban poverty in terms of the spillover effect of rural poverty has been challenged, indicating that the elasticity of urban poverty with respect to rural poverty is only nominal (Mitra, 1994; and Mills and Mitra, 1997). Papola (1981) and Banerjee (1986) find no evidence to support the notion that migrants are predominantly located in the informal service sector. Mohan (1979) also notes that migrants in Bogota were not disadvantaged in comparison to the natives and that the incidence of poverty was similar among both the groups. On the whole, studies suggest considerable improvements in living standards after migration from the rural to the urban areas, supporting Kuznets' (1966) upward income mobility hypothesis involving locational (rural-urban), occupational, and industrial shifts of the individuals and their incomes along with the availability of progressively better economic opportunities. Policy makers and journalists, however, as mentioned above, continue to regard slums as the homes of the vulnerable groups; they make no serious attempt to understand the reasons behind the success stories that many of these households may reveal on closer examination. This short-sighted and superficial perspective prompted the present study to analyse the living standards of households in the slums of Delhi.

The organization of the chapter is as follows. The next section examines some of the broad indicators of the living standards in slum clusters. Section 5.3 identifies the major determinants of living standards, focusing on the network variable which controls the decision to migrate, labour market choices, and living conditions in the place of destination. Section 5.4 examines the health status of the slum dwellers and the main findings are summarized in Section 5.5.

5.2 Broad Patterns

It is interesting to note that the level of inequality, as measured in terms of the Gini coefficient, is closer to the city-level inequality.[1] On the other hand, the incidence of poverty, i.e. the percentage of the population below the poverty line, is estimated at 25 per cent, which is higher than the poverty ratio at the city level (8.23 per cent, 1999–2000). In the popular literature slums are usually treated as being inhabited by the urban poor. From this point of view, an incidence of poverty of only 25 per cent appears to be on the low side. In the slum survey of the NSS (1976–7), around 40 per cent of the slum population in Delhi was found to be below the poverty line. Two sets of questions arise in relation to these findings: (1) who are the inhabitants of these slums if poor households do not reside there? and (2) where do the urban poor live if not in slums?

The second question is easy to answer. Slum households considered in our study are primarily taken from the clusters which, as mentioned above, are recognized slums. In other words, these clusters enjoy a more or less legal status, and have existed in the city for a considerably long period. At the most slum dwellers are relocated within the city but are not pushed out of the city. The vulnerable lots are perhaps not able to seek an entry to these slums in their search for accommodation. They continue to reside illegally in unauthorized colonies, marginal settlements, pavements, and other public places. A detailed analysis of only those who are able to reach the authorized slums is carried out in this chapter.

In order to answer the first question we would require a detailed analysis of the socio-economic profile of the slum dwellers. The point that we emphasize here is that poverty is not insignificant even in these authorized slums if the households are taken in isolation from each other. Several informal mechanisms of support that exist and operate subtly among the households allow many of them to escape poverty and cope with the risks arising from occupational and/or income instability, poor health status, and inadequate amenities such as drinking water, sanitation, and sewerage. We have already noted the importance of the network variable in accessing employment opportunities and experiencing an upward occupational mobility. In this chapter we identify other variables in terms of access to NGOs, voter's identity/public distribution system card, short/long distance migrants, natives versus short/long duration migrants, nature of employment/occupation, household composition, caste, and location-specific factors in determining the standard of living. The most popular approach to the analysis of the standard of living is based on the per capita consumption expenditure per month though other aspects of the standard of living can be captured by examining the quality of housing in which the slum dwellers reside, and their health status. A preliminary look at the distribution of households against per capita household expenditure shows that about 25 per cent of the households fall into the category of Rs. 0–625 per month. The poverty line for 1993–4 was estimated at Rs. 309 for Delhi urban (see Malhotra, 1997), which if inflated by the consumer price index for industrial workers turns out to be Rs. 570 for 1999–2000. While around one-fifth of the households are estimated to be below the poverty line, another one-fourth appear to be just above the poverty line.

Table 5.1 gives the distribution of households by household size and per capita expenditure size classes. Large households are usually located in lower expenditure size classes. Around 44 per cent of the households with a size of 6 and above are in the range of Rs. 0–625 per month expenditure per capita. In fact, it is quite evident from Table 5.1 that with an increase in household size the percentage of households falling into the size class that comprises the poverty line and the size classes below the poverty line also increases steadily. Not even one single-member household is seen below the poverty line. Food expenditure per capita and household size reveals this more prominently (Table 5.2). Around 75 per cent of the households in the expenditure group Rs. 0 to Rs. 275 per month have at least six members in the household. Similarly, around 50 per cent of

TABLE 5.1: PERCENTAGE DISTRIBUTION OF HOUSEHOLDS BY PER CAPITA CONSUMPTION EXPENDITURE SIZE CLASSES AND HOUSEHOLD SIZE

Per Capita Cons. Exp. Size Class (Rs.)	Household Size						Total
	1	2	3	4	5	6 and above	
<Rs. 275	0.0	1.6	0.0	0.0	0.0	1.8	0.7
275–449	0.0	0.0	3.2	3.4	7.0	13.7	7.6
450–624	0.0	3.3	9.5	12.2	13.9	28.5	17.2
625–799	0.0	11.5	16.8	22.4	21.9	27.5	22.2
800–974	7.1	9.8	16.8	21.8	21.9	10.5	16.1
975–1,149	7.1	22.9	22.1	15.6	14.9	9.5	14.5
1,150 and above	85.7	50.8	31.6	24.5	20.4	8.5	21.7
Total	100.0	100.0	100.0	100.0	100.0	100.0	100.0
	(1.7)	(7.6)	(11.8)	(18.3)	(25.1)	(35.4)	

Note: Each column adds up to 100 per cent. Figures in parentheses add up to 100 per cent.

the households in the expenditure group Rs. 275 to Rs. 450 reside in households with at least six members. It is interesting to note that the mean per capita monthly expenditure and the mean per capita income are almost the same for the slum households, indicating almost zero savings on an average. However, our econometric analysis in the next section identifies the determinants of the ability to save and the housing type, and explains the variations in per capita expenditure per month.

In Chapter 3 we examined the cross-classification of workers in accordance with their income and occupation. In this chapter we investigate the cross-classification of individuals by the expenditure per capita and the occupations of the working persons, and the non-working persons (Table 5.3). Incidence of poverty is least among the professionals (12.7 per cent). Interestingly, workers in personal services again registered an incidence of only 18 per cent—about 7 percentage points less than that of the figure corresponding to all individuals—though they are usually believed to be in the lower rungs. This could be due to the non-monetary support that these workers receive from their employers in spite of their supposedly low earnings. Support from the employers can range from the supply of food and clothing to medical reimbursement when the workers fall ill. As we have sought to convert such non-financial support into monetary terms while calculating the household expenditure, it is possible that the workers reported a lower incidence of poverty than what one may usually expect. All this evidence tends to highlight the fact that transactions take place between the employers and employees outside the standard practices of the labour market, and hence an analysis of the labour market without reference to these informal support mechanisms would offer only an incomplete picture of the actual payment that workers receive. The actual income in the urban labour market tends to be underestimated if sufficient care is not taken to capture these non-standard aspects of payment.

Even among the sales workers around 20 per cent are found below the poverty line, though one would have expected a much larger figure. Surprisingly, the percentage of workers in commercial services lying below the poverty line is almost similar to what is noted at the aggregate level, that is 25 per cent. Since these activities in commercial services are believed to offer high-income jobs such an estimate is possibly the outcome of a larger dependency ratio. Second, some of the jobs in commercial services actually offer low incomes.

TABLE 5.2: DISTRIBUTION OF HOUSEHOLDS ACROSS PER CAPITA FOOD EXPENDITURE AND HOUSEHOLD SIZE

Per (Rs.) Capita Food Exp. Per Month	Household Size							Total
	1	2	3	4	5	6	7 and above	
0–275	0.0	0.0	3.8	1.9	18.9	20.7	54.7	100 (6.6)
275–450	0.4	2.8	10.6	13.0	23.2	24.8	25.2	100 (30.7)
450–625	0.4	5.6	9.6	21.1	31.9	19.1	12.3	100 (31.3)
625–800	1.3	15.9	16.6	22.8	23.6	11.5	8.3	100 (19.6)
800–975	0.0	4.5	25.0	27.3	22.7	4.5	15.9	100 (5.5)
975–1,150	11.4	25.7	8.6	31.4	20.0	2.9	0.0	100 (4.4)
1,150–1,325	25.0	12.5	12.5	0.0	37.5	12.5	0.0	100 (1.0)
1,325–1,500	50.0	25.0	12.5	0.0	0.0	12.5	0.0	100 (1.0)
Total	1.7	7.5	11.7	18.1	25.4	17.8	17.7	100

Note: Each row adds up to 100 per cent. Figures in parentheses add up to 100 per cent across the last column.

TABLE 5.3: PERCENTAGE DISTRIBUTION OF POPULATION BY OCCUPATION AND PER CAPITA EXPENDITURE SIZE CLASSES

Per Capita Expenditure Size Class	Occupation												Total
	Non-Workers	Pro-fess-ional	Sales	Trade	Per-sonal Service	Manu-factur-ing	Commer-cial Service	Trans-port	Tailor-ing	Const-ruction	Secu-rity	Repair-ing	
<275	1.2	0.0	0.6	0.0	0.6	0.0	1.5	0.0	0.0	2.8	0.0	2.0	1.1
275–449	10.4	5.8	6.2	10.8	10.1	6.0	8.0	10.0	5.9	10.4	10.0	10.4	9.9
450–624	21.9	10.1	19.9	16.8	12.4	24.8	23.3	22.5	23.5	19.4	30.0	16.7	20.9
625–799	24.0	18.8	22.4	17.3	27.8	30.8	18.9	15.0	23.5	24.6	0.0	14.6	23.5
800–974	15.3	14.5	14.3	17.8	16.0	11.1	16.1	5.0	20.6	16.0	10.0	0.0	15.1
975–1,149	12.4	13.0	13.7	14.6	14.2	6.8	18.2	27.5	14.7	10.4	0.0	18.7	12.8
1,150 +	14.7	37.7	23.0	22.7	18.9	20.5	13.9	20.0	11.8	16.3	50.0	37.5	16.6
Total	100.0	100.0	100.0	100.0	100.0	100.0	100.0	100.0	100.0	100.0	100.0	100.0	100.0
	(68.6)	(1.7)	(4.0)	(4.6)	(4.2)	(2.9)	(3.4)	(1.0)	(0.8)	(7.2)	(0.2)	(1.2)	

Note: Each column adds up to 100 per cent. Figures in parentheses across the row adds up to 100 per cent.

In the construction sector, despite relatively higher earnings, the incidence of poverty is as high as that among the non-workers (around 27 per cent). This could be due to the high propensity to save exhibited by workers in this sector. As construction activities are usually seasonal, and since many of these workers come temporarily to the city to earn money, their inclination to minimize their expenditure on consumption is quite strong.

5.3 Econometric Analysis

In this exercise we try to explain the variations in per capita total expenditure per month for the sample households (PCE). Besides, in alternative formulations the quality of housing (QHH) and the ability to save (SAVE) are also used as dependent variables.

The explanatory variables are as follows: household size (HHSZ), gender of the household head (GEND, 0 for males and 1 for females), proportion of the number of children in the age group 0–14 to the total number of household members in the household (PCHILD), duration of migration in terms of the number of years spent in the city with a value of 0 for the non-migrants (DMIG), dummy with a value of 1 for those who are literate and 0 for illiterates (EDUC), dummy differentiating between short- and long-distance migrants from the natives (SDMIG and LDMIG respectively), CAST dummy representing 1 for scheduled caste and scheduled tribe population and 0 otherwise, TOK dummy taking a value of 1 for having access to token or voter's identity or ration card and 0 otherwise, and NGO re-presenting the accessibility of the household to the services of non-government organizations (1 and 0 for positive and negative response respectively). Besides, six zone-pecific dummies are considered as the city of Delhi has been divided into seven zones in total. The income of the household head or the principal earner (HHINC) is also taken as a determinant of the standard of living. In some of the alternate specifications we have considered the nature of employment dummies or occupation dummies instead of the income of the principal earner. As there are three types of employment considered in the survey, two dummies for self-employment (SELF = 1, 0 otherwise) and regular-wage or salaried employment (RSAL = 1, 0 otherwise) have been included, casual employment being the reference category. Similarly ten occupation specific dummies (OCCP i, = 0–9) are considered, repair services (OCCP10) being the reference group.

Among the female-headed households—where the principal earner is a woman—the standard of living is expected to be lower than that of the male-headed households as labour market discrimination yields lower earnings for female workers compared to male workers. With an increase in the percentage of children in the household, per capita consumption may actually rise as many of them join the labour market directly or indirectly and augment the family income. Since their volume of consumption is less than that of an adult, their participation in the labour market even with their meagre earnings tends to raise rather than reduce the standard of living in per capita terms. Among the scheduled castes/scheduled tribes, the standards of living are usually believed to be lower than those of others as they may not qualify for high-income jobs due to the lack of skill.

With education and with accessibility to a token indicating ownership of property or a voter's identity or a ration card and to the services provided by the NGOs, the standard of living is expected to improve. Long duration migrants are supposed to be better off than short duration migrants because of their familiarity with the urban job market. With income—or alternately employment/occupation categories which are expected to provide stable jobs and regular income—per capita expenditure is likely to increase. The question whether short-distance migrants are better off as compared to the long-distance migrants or otherwise can only be resolved on the basis of empirical evidence. The regression equations have been estimated in the light of these variations. Access to certain types of clusters endowed with basic amenities is possible only through contacts. In this respect certain communities or groups with specific regional/cultural backgrounds operate more prominently than the rest; it is expected that with some of these factors will be captured by the zone-specific dummies. In other words, the significance of the zone-specific dummies can bring out the differences in the standards of living that can be attributed to location-specific advantages/disadvantages and to the cultural factors of the groups residing in these areas.

The two other dependent variables taken in alternate formulations are as follows: quality of housing is taken in terms of three categories of roofs: (a) thatched/card/plastic, (b) asbestos/tin and, (c) brick/stone/tile. For this, a multinomial logit model has been estimated. Households responding to the questoin whether they have savings in any form (1 for positive and 0 for negative response) have been analysed in a binomial logit framework.

The empirical results reported in Table 5.4 can be summarized as follows: in the equation for per capita consumption expenditure one of the variables which is highly significant is household size, which reduces the standard of living. Literates appear to be better off as compared to those who are illiterate. With an increase in the percentage of children it is confirmed that consumption expenditure per capita increases, which indirectly tends to confirm the participation of children in the labour market, though in the last chapter we did not note any significant evidence in favour of child labour. Income of the household head has a positive effect on consumption per capita. Interestingly, access to a token, etc., does not seem to raise the standard of living; rather it lowers the per capita expenditure. This is possibly because households with access to a token or a voter's identity card or a ration card make investments in housing, which could at times be at the cost of consumption expenditure. Instead of income if we consider the employment categories in terms of dummies, those who are in regular-wage or salaried jobs appear to have a lower consumption expenditure per capita while that of the self-employed is not different from that of the casual workers. The possible reason for this might be that if the household head is engaged in stable employment the probability of the other members joining the labour market is low, and hence the consumption expenditure tends to be adversely affected. Occupation-wise though we noted in the last section that the incidence of poverty among those engaged in personal services is rather on the low side—contrary to the general belief. The regression results show that on an average the consumption per capita is lower in the household if the head is engaged in personal services. The dummy for construction also takes a negative sign. Across space, Zones 2 and 4 are found to have lower standards of living compared to the rest.

The results of the multinomial logit model for types of housing show that literates are less likely to reside in the first category of houses which are the worst type or the most temporary type in terms of construction materials (Table 5.5). With an increase in income the probability again drops. Zones 1, 3, 4, 5, and 6 also take negative coefficients. The long-distance migrants are more likely to reside in these slums, possibly because they are less endowed in terms of information relating to space for housing. Encroachments in pure illegal space would obviously discourage any substantive investment in housing. Besides, if long-distance migrants are more vulnerable in

TABLE 5.4: REGRESSION RESULTS FOR PER CAPITA TOTAL EXPENDITURE (OLS ESTIMATION)
DEP VAR: PER CAPITA TOTAL EXPENDITURE PER MONTH (PCE)

	Equation 1		Equation 2		Equation 3	
HHSZ	-117.34	(-12.45)*	-95.19	(-10.69)*	-95.06	(10.70)*
DMIG	44.93	(0.82)	46.83	(0.84)	41.85	(0.75)
EDUC	90.59	(2.97)*	80.67	(2.58)*	73.40	(2.33)*
GEND	16.39	(0.26)	-3.33	(-0.05)	20.03	(0.31)
PCHILD	1.98	(2.75)*	0.68	(0.98)	0.51	(0.74)
HHINC	0.04	(6.25)*				
CAST	27.48	(-0.92)	-23.01	(-0.74)	-15.27	(-0.49)
ZONE1	-22.22	(-0.36)	-23.34	(-0.37)	-18.50	(-0.29)
ZONE2	-137.53	(-1.88)**	-135.53	(-1.81)**	-129.61	(-1.73)**
ZONE3	-43.62	(-0.68)	-36.30	(-0.56)	-30.33	(-0.47)
ZONE4	-146.97	(-2.32)*	-148.06	(-2.29)*	-144.17	(-2.23)*
ZONE5	-62.87	(-0.95)	-71.66	(-1.07)	-81.59	(-1.20)
ZONE6	-68.80	(-0.81)	-69.98	(-0.81)	-80.12	(-0.93)
NGO	63.96	(1.17)	64.55	(1.16)	59.25	(1.07)
TOKEN	-265.77	(-4.31)	297.78	(-4.73)*	-288.44	(-4.56)*
SDMIG	-16.06	(-0.20)	-38.58	(-0.47)	-42.80	(-0.52)
LDMIG	59.23	(0.71)	70.44	(0.83)	65.60	(0.77)
SELF			29.48	(0.79)		
RSAL			-113.67	(-3.06)*		
OCCP0					58.99	(0.58)
OCCP1					-151.70	(-1.65)**
OCCP2					-69.22	(-0.78)

(contd.)

TABLE 5.4 (contd.)

	Equation 1		Equation 2		Equation 3	
OCCP3					-280.85	(-2.80)*
OCCP4					-117.65	(-1.24)
OCCP5					-80.11	(-0.87)
OCCP6					-9.27	(-0.08)
OCCP7					-11.49	(-0.09)
OCCP8					-187.47	(-2.18)*
OCCP9					-103.15	(-0.58)
INTERCEPT	1,496.59	(11.79)*	1,648.31	(12.52)*	1,719.04	(11.49)
R^2		0.26		0.24		0.24
N		800		800		800

Notes: Figures in parentheses give t-ratios. The asterisk marks *, **, and *** represent significance at the 5, 10, and 20 per cent levels respectively.

OCCP0 = professionals, OCCP1 = sales workers, OCCP2 = trade workers, OCCP3 = personal services, OCCP4 = manufacturing, OCCP5 = commercial services, OCCP6 = transport, OCCP7 = tailoring, etc., OCCP8 = construction, OCCP9 = security workers, OCCP10 = repairing

TABLE 5.5: REGRESSION RESULTS FOR QUALITY OF HOUSING (MODEL: MULTINOMIAL LOGIT, MAX LIKELIHOOD ESTIMATION) *DEP VAR: QUALITY OF HOUSING*

	Equation 1				Equation 2				Equation 3			
	0		1		0		1		0		1	
HHSZ	0.05	(0.81)	-0.04	(-0.73)	-0.03	(-0.48)	-0.12	-(2.01)*	-0.010	(-0.16)	-0.10	(-1.80)**
DMIG	0.48	(1.22)	0.22	(0.64)	0.32	(0.78)	0.12	(0.36)	0.44	(1.06)	0.14	(0.39)
EDUC	-0.78	(-3.73)*	-0.23	(-1.20)	-0.66	(-3.08)*	-0.20	(-1.02)	-0.64	(-2.93)*	-0.23	(-1.17)
GEND	-0.20	(-0.49)	-0.32	(-0.79)	-0.05)	(-0.13)	-0.26	(-0.65)	-0.02	(-0.05)	-0.23	(-0.55)
PCHILD	0.004	(0.77)	0.007	(1.48)***	0.008	(1.72)**	0.01	(2.44)*	0.007	(1.54)***	0.01	(2.40)
HHINC	-0.0001	(-2.70)*	-0.0001	(-2.52)*								
CAST	0.27	(1.30)***	0.19	(1.05)	0.34	(1.57)***	0.25	(1.31)***	0.30	(1.38)***	0.23	(1.20)
ZONE 1	-1.95	(-4.45)*	-0.21	(-0.44)	-1.86	(-4.14)*	-0.15	(-0.30)	-2.05	(-4.46)*	-0.18	(-0.37)
ZONE 2	0.03	(0.06)	0.61	(0.98)	0.18	(0.32)	0.69	(1.11)	-0.04	(-0.07)	0.65	(1.05)
ZONE 3	-2.74	(-5.98)*	-0.95	(-1.95)**	-2.74	(-5.87)*	-0.92	(-1.89)**	-2.96	(-6.22)*	-0.98	(-2.00)*
ZONE 4	-2.75	(-5.65)*	0.23	(0.47)	-2.74	(-5.55)*	0.25	(0.51)	-2.90	(-5.76)*	0.23	(0.48)
ZONE 5	-3.14	(-6.70)*	-1.96	(3.78)	-3.03	(-6.38)*	-1.89	(-3.65)*	-3.09	(6.33)*	-1.84	(-3.49)*
ZONE 6	-3.44	(-5.15)*	-2.01	(3.14)*	-3.38	(-4.93)*	-1.92	(-2.99)*	-3.63	(-5.25)*	-1.98	(-3.08)*
NGO	-0.45	(-1.17)	-0.33	(-0.99)	-0.34	(-0.88)	-0.30	(-0.91)	-0.29	(-0.75)	-0.31	(-0.90)
TOKEN	-0.09	(0.20)	-0.14	(-0.38)	0.26	(0.58)	-0.03	(-0.07)	0.38	(0.82)	0.03	(0.07)
SDMIG	0.17	(0.26)	-0.31	(-0.63)	0.40	(0.63)	0.14	(-0.29)	0.24	(0.36)	-0.28	(-0.55)
LDMIG	0/90	(1.38)***	-0.24	(-0.47)	0.94	(1.43)***	-0.18	(-0.36)	0.81	(1.19)	-0.27	(-0.52)
SELF					0.45	(1.73)**	0.26	(1.16)				
RSAL					1.38	(5.34)*	0.72	(3.07)*				
OCCP0									-1.13	(1.39)***	-0.49	(0.82)
OCCP1									1.02	(1.52)***	0.20	(0.36)

(contd.)

TABLE 5.5 (contd.)

	Equation 1				Equation 2				Equation 3			
	0		1		0		1		0		1	
OCCP2									-0.42	(-0.65)	-0.35	(-0.66)
OCCP3									0.04	(0.06)	-0.33	(-0.56)
OCCP4									0.02	(0.03)	0.09	(0.15)
OCCP5									-0.75	(-1.07)	-0.70	(-1.28)***
OCCP6									0.45	(0.56)	-0.15	(-0.22)
OCCP7									-0.19	(-0.21)	0.12	(0.17)
OCCP8									0.81	(1.28)***	0.16	(0.32)
OCCP9									1.30	(0.91)	0.93	(0.75)
INTERCEPT	1.28	(1.40)***	1.37	(1.62)***	0.09	(0.10)	0.65)	(0.76)	0.49	(0.45)	1.06	(1.10)
N	798				798				798			

Notes: 1. Category 2 is the comparison group in each of the three equations.
2. Figures in parentheses give t ratios. The asterisk marks *, ** and *** represent significance at the 5, 10, and 20 per cent levels respectively.
3. Chi-square values for the three equations are 256.56, 276.95, and 290.65 respectively, which are significant at the 1 per cent level.

the job market compared to the short-distance migrants, it would again lead to the growth of poor-quality housing. In terms of employment categories, it is evident that regular-wage or salaried employees are less likely to reside in these slum houses. The occupation dummies, on the other hand, show that professionals have a lower probability of residing in these slums, while the sales workers show a higher probability. Scheduled castes are also more likely to reside in these slums than others. With an increase in the percentage of children, households show a higher probability of landing in this worst category of slums.

On the other hand, as far as the second category of housing (roof built with asbestos/tin sheets) is concerned, income again takes a negative coefficient, indicating that households with higher income are more likely to reside in the third category of slums, that is, *pucca* slums. In terms of areas, zones 3, 5, and 6 show a lower probability of locating such a type of slums. When we replace income by nature of employment dummies the coefficient of the dummy for regular-wage jobs turns out to be positive and significant, indicating an increase in the probability of residing in this category of slums. In this equation the household size takes a negative coefficient, implying that large households are less likely to stay in this type of slums. Since household size is not a significant variable in the equation for the first category of slums, we may interpret that with an increase in the size of the household the willingness to invest in housing also increases, and hence the probability of residing in the third category of slums increases. However, with an increase in the percentage of children within the household, the probability of staying in the second category of slums shoots up. So it is only when the household size increases with the addition of more adult members rather than additions due to the birth of children that the quality of housing seems to improve. More or less similar findings emerge when we replace the nature of employment dummies by the occupation dummies though none of these dummies turns out to be significant in the equation for the second category of slums.

Finally, as we estimate a binomial logit model for those who can save and those who cannot save, irrespective of the nature or the amount of savings, the following results are obtained (Table 5.6). With an increase in the duration of migration the probability of not saving declines, implying that the long-duration migrants are more likely to save. Similarly, with increse in the levels of literacy and income the likelihood of saving also rises. Households which have access to services provided by NGOs are also more likely to save. The long-distance migrants are less likely to save as compared to the short-distance migrants and the natives. As income is replaced by the nature of employment dummies, it is interesting to note that household heads in regular-wage employment are less likely to save. This is quite surprising but it could be due to the fact, as mentioned earlier, that the less uncertain jobs of the heads perhaps keep the other members of the household outside the labour market. Hence, total income and saving per household drops. Occupations such as commercial services and transport hold the possibility of higher rates of saving. Across space, those in Zone 1 are more likely to save compared to their counterparts in the other zones. On the whole, the findings regarding the standards of living reveal several new characteristics, which are at times contrary to the conventional wisdom.

5.4 Health

An analysis of the living standard would remain incomplete if we do not refer to the health status of the slum population. The close nexus between poverty and health needs to be understood before effective policy measures can be suggested (Dreze and Sen, 1989). Between the two, which one is the cause and which the effect is unclear; whether poor health is due to a poor standard of living or whether meagre earnings are the outcome of poor health conditions is a complex question to which there is no easy answer. However, both factors seem to mutually reinforce each other.

The slum dwellers were asked to report two major illnesses suffered in the last one year. In regard to the first major illness the incidence of illness is slightly more than 8 per cent. These illnesses do not relate to the common cold or to fever; illnesses including accidents which prolonged for some time (and in the case of workers caused income losses) have been reported. It may be noted that among those who are unwell, about 55 per cent are either not in the job market (and hence are dependents) or are unemployed. Second, around 40 per cent of the ill population is found to be suffering from liver- and stomach-related diseases (Table 5.7). At least 30 per cent of the workers in sales, personal services, manufacturing, tailoring, and construction suffered from liver-related problems. Though it is diffi-

TABLE 5.6: REGRESSION RESULTS FOR SAVING (MODEL: BINOMIAL LOGIT, MAX LIKELIHOOD ESTIMATION) *DEP VAR: SAVING*

	Equation 1		Equation 2		Equation 3	
HHSZ	0.05	(0.86)	-0.50	(-1.03)	-0.04	(-0.83)
DMIG	-0.63	(-2.21)*	-0.62	(-2.18)*	-0.70	(-2.44)*
EDUC	-0.59	(-3.60)*	-0.59	(-3.58)	-0.58	(-3.45)*
GEND	0.01	(0.04)	0.08	(0.24)	-0.05	(-0.14)
PCHILD	0.001	(0.35)	0.01	(1.97)*	0.008	(2.16)*
HHINC	-0.0002	(-3.95)*				
CAST	0.15	(0.94)	0.13	0.78	0.11	(0.64)
ZONE1	-0.90	(-2.66)*	-0.91	(-2.70)*	-0.88	(-2.58)*
ZONE2	-0.22	(-0.58)	-0.21	(-0.54)	-0.16	(-0.42)
ZONE3	-0.34	(-1.01)	-0.37	(-1.09)	-0.33	(0.96)
ZONE4	0.083	(-0.25)	-0.09	(-0.27)	-0.07	(-0.22)
ZONE5	-0.40	(-1.14)	-0.38	(1.11)	-0.22	(-0.61)
ZONE6	0.03	(0.07)	0.03	(0.07)	0.15	(0.34)
NGO	-0.72	(-2.01)*	-0.74	(-2.09)*	-0.73	(-2.04)*
TOKEN	-0.32	(-1.00)	-0.22	(-0.69)	-0.18	(-0.55)
SDMIG	0.48	(1.11)	0.54	(1.26)	0.60	(1.38)***
LDMIG	0.70	(1.56)***	0.66	(1.49)***	0.71	(1.58)***
SELF			-0.09	(-0.46)		
RSAL			0.32	(-1.65)**		
OCCP0					-0.58	(-1.04)
OCCP1					0.008	(0.02)
OCCP2					-0.40	(-0.87)

(contd.)

TABLE 5.6 (contd.)

	Equation 1		Equation 2		Equation 3	
OCCP3					0.31	(0.60)
OCCP4					-0.06	(-0.11)
OCCP5					-0.72	(-1.47)***
OCCP6					-0.87	(-1.33)***
OCCP7					-0.094	(0.14)
OCCP8					0.17	(0.39)
OCCP9					0.72	(0.81)
INTERCEPT	0.55	(0.81)	-0.075	(-0.11)	0.11	(0.15)
N	801		801		801	

Notes: 1. Between 0 and 1 the latter is the comparison group.

2. Figures in parentheses give t ratios. The asterisk marks *, **, and *** represent significance at the 5, 10, and 20 perc ent levels respectively.

3. Chi-square values for the three equations are 65.97, 49.88, and 63.77 respectively. They are all significant at the 1 per cent level.

cult to suggest any clear-cut connection between occupations and the diseases from which the slum-dwelling workers suffer, occupations such as trade and construction alone comprise around 40 per cent of the total working population which has been unwell.

It is well known that diseases in low-income households usually go unreported unless they involve major expenditure and/or loss of income due to absence from work. As health expenditure is usually incurred by these households as a residual category after meeting the most important needs relating to food, clothing, and shelter, and as many of them cannot afford to undergo any major loss of income by remaining absent from work for long, reported illnesses are a gross under-estimate of the reality. In fact, the general health condition in slums is so poor that the slum dweller's perception about illness is quite different from that of a researcher, and hence an analysis of illness data is far from being complete or realistic.

Notwithstanding the limitations of information pertaining to illness, the close associations between poor standards of living and poor health status are quite evident. One important manifestation of poor health status is the high fertility rate to compensate for the high rates of mortality and morbidity. The age distribution of the slum population shows that around 40 per cent belong to the age bracket 0–14, which is indicative of a high fertility rate.

An important interconnection between poor health conditions and the standard of living is undernutrition, and we note that a large percentage of the slum clusters are located in low/moderate expenditure size classes with reference to the poverty line. Although many of the workers have access to jobs with reasonably good earnings, as noted in the previous chapter, per capita expenditure is considerably low for a large number of households, mainly due to the large size of the household. The distribution of the ill population by illness type and expenditure size classes given in Table 5.8 shows that blood pressure related illnesses are suffered mostly by the poor. Poor also account for about 40 per cent of accident-related illnesses. Besides, a sizeable number of the total deformity- and fracture-related cases are reported from the poor households. On the whole, the illness patterns of the poor and the non-poor even within the slum clusters is somewhat different. Hence, expenditure patterns and health status cannot be taken to be unrelated. In an earlier study by Gupta and Mitra (1998) noted that those incurring expenditure on a nutritious diet were less likely to fall sick compared to those who could not spend on such food and drink.

TABLE 5.7: PERCENTAGE DISTRIBUTION OF INDIVIDUALS BY NON-WORKERS, WORKERS, AND ILLNESS TYPE

	Accident	Stomach-Related Problem	Heart-Related Disease	Epidemic	Gynaecological Problem	Mental Illness	Fracture	Blood Pressure-Related Problem	Liver-Related Problem
Non-workers	1.6	16.8	3.3	5.4	7.6	2.2	3.8	1.1	26.1
Professional	7.7	23.1	0.0	0.0	7.7	7.7	7.7	0.0	15.4
Sales	0.0	5.9	5.9	0.0	0.0	5.9	0.0	0.0	29.4
Trade	7.7	19.2	0.0	3.8	0.0	7.7	3.8	3.8	7.7
Personal Service	0.0	16.7	11.2	0.0	7.7	0.0	5.5	0.0	33.3
Manufacturing	5.9	5.9	0.0	0.0	7.7	0.0	0.0	0.0	41.2
Commercial Service	7.7	30.8	0.0	0.0	0.0	15.4	0.0	0.0	23.1
Transport	0.0	0.0	25.0	0.0	0.0	0.0	0.0	0.0	25.0
Tailoring	0.0	0.0	0.0	0.0	0.0	0.0	0.0	0.0	66.7
Construction	3.3	16.7	3.3	3.3	0.0	0.0	0.0	6.7	33.3
Security	0.0	0.0	0.0	0.0	0.0	0.0	0.0	0.0	0.0
Repairing	16.7	0.0	16.7	0.0	0.0	0.0	16.7	0.0	16.7
Total	3.02	16.1	3.6	3.6	5.1	3.02	3.3	1.5	26.3

(contd.)

TABLE 5.7 (contd.)

	Lung-Related Illness	Body Ache	Burn Injury	Cancer	Ear, Nose and Throat Problem	Kidney-Related Problem	Deformity	Ill Pop. as % of Total
Non-worker	13.0	6.0	6.5	0.5	2.2	2.2	1.6	6.7
Professional	23.1	0.0	7.7	0.0	0.0	0.0	0.0	18.8
Sales	17.6	5.9	11.8	0.0	11.8	5.9	0.0	10.6
Trade	26.9	3.8	11.5	0.0	3.8	0.0	0.0	14.1
Personal Service	5.5	11.1	11.1	0.0	0.0	0.0	0.0	10.7
Manufacturing	23.5	11.8	5.9	0.0	0.0	0.0	0.0	14.5
Commercial Service	15.4	7.7	0.0	0.0	0.0	0.0	0.0	9.5
Transport	0.0	25.0	0.0	0.0	25.0	0.0	0.0	10.0
Tailoring	0.0	0.0	33.3	0.0	0.0	0.0	0.0	8.8
Construction	2.0	3.3	6.7	0.0	0.0	3.3	0.0	10.4
Security	0.0	0.0	0.0	0.0	0.0	0.0	0.0	0.0
Repairing	16.7	16.7	0.0	0.0	0.0	0.0	0.0	12.5
Total	1.54	6.3	7.2	0.3	2.4	1.8	0.9	8.3

Note: Figures in each row except the last column add up to 100 per cent.

TABLE 5.8: PERCENTAGE DISTRIBUTION OF POPULATION BY ILLNESSES AND MONTHLY PER CAPITA EXPENDITURE (Rs.) SIZE CLASSES

Illnesses	Per Capita Expenditure Size Classes							Total
	<275	275–449	450–624	625–799	800–974	975–1,149	1,150 and above	
Accident	0.0	10.0	30.0	10.0	0.0	0.0	50.0	100.0
Stomach	0.0	1.9	7.5	18.7	26.4	13.2	32.1	100.0
Heart	0.0	0.0	0.0	0.0	16.7	25.0	58.3	100.0
Epidemic	0.0	8.3	0.0	33.3	41.7	0.0	16.7	100.0
Gynaecological	0.0	0.0	0.0	23.5	5.9	11.8	58.8	100.0
Mental	0.0	10.0	20.0	20.0	20.0	10.0	20.0	100.0
Fracture	0.0	0.0	27.3	36.4	9.1	18.2	9.1	100.0
Blood Pressure	0.0	60.0	40.0	0.0	0.0	0.0	0.0	100.0
Liver	0.0	2.3	12.6	25.3	17.2	14.9	27.6	100.0
Lungs	0.0	7.8	17.6	29.4	9.8	5.9	29.4	100.0
Body Ache	0.0	4.8	14.3	33.3	19.0	9.5	19.0	100.0
Cancer	0.0	0.0	0.0	100.0	0.0	0.0	0.0	100.0
ENT	0.0	0.0	12.5	25.0	25.0	0.0	37.5	100.0
Kidney	0.0	16.7	0.0	16.7	33.3	0.0	33.0	100.0
Deformity	0.0	0.0	33.3	0.0	0.0	0.0	66.7	100.0
Burns	0.0	0.0	20.8	29.2	16.7	80.3	25.0	100.0

Note: Each row adds up to 100 per cent.

On the whole, we note the poor health conditions of the slum dwellers, particularly in certain occupations, though the incidence of illness among the total population does not turn out to be high. But this is mainly because of under-reporting. Second, the interconnection between expenditure per capita (or the standard of living) and health conditions exist, suggesting the significance of an effective and target-oriented health policy in dealing with the problem of slums and urban poverty.

5.5 Conclusion

In this chapter we have examined the standard of living of the slum population in Delhi. Though one would expect a very large incidence of poverty among slum dwellers, the estimate is rather on the low side. This could be because we have considered only the registered slums in the city. The unregistered/illegal squatter settlements not covered in our study might well be the home of the vulnerable lot. However, it is to be noted that even within these registered slums the percentage of the population marginally above the poverty line is quite large, though the incidence of poverty did not appear to be high.

We have several interesting features about the determinants of the standards of living. Differences across space within the city in the standards of living, either in terms of per capita consumption expenditure or the quality of housing or the ability to save, are quite prominent. With an increse in the income of the household head, the standard of living in terms of per capita expenditure improves. Given the percentage of children within the household, with an increase in household size—which implies additions in terms of adults, and not simply due to a high fertility rate—the quality of housing tends to improve. However, with an increase in the proportion of children the per capita expenditure also increases instead of declining, though the latter case is usually expected. The increase could be due to the contribution made by child labour in augmenting the family income and thus the expenditure in per capita terms. Female-headed households are worse off compared to male-headed households in terms of per capita consumption expenditure. Relationships between occupations and/or employment categories and standards of living are noteworthy, and hence it would be misleading to characterize all activities within the informal sector by low productivity. The significance of the zone-specific dummies, particularly in the equations for the quality of housing, again indicates the heterogeneity in living standards interspatially. The effect of caste on the quality of housing is not insignificant either; the scheduled castes usually reside in poor-quality housing. The impact of education on both quality of housing and per capita expenditure is positive. The interconnection between health conditions and per capita expenditure is also quite prominent, suggesting the vulnerability in terms of health conditions of those located in the lower rungs of the socio-economic ladder.

NOTE

1. The Gini coefficient based on our slum survey (1999–2000) turns out to be 0.28, which is more or less similar to what was noted in the National Sample Survey on slum dwellers in Delhi (0.2736 in 1976–7). In urban Delhi the level of inequality was 0.2812 in 1977–8; see Mitra (1990).

CHAPTER 6

INTER-HOUSEHOLD TRANSFER OF RESOURCES

6.1 Introduction

In the preceding chapters we noted that networks play a significant role in allowing migrants to access information on the urban job market and to attain occupational mobility, which bring in considerable improvement in their standards of living. Finding shelter in slums endowed with basic amenities is also possible through contacts. In this chapter we examine the issue of transfers and remittances, which happen to benefit a much larger proportion of the population than merely the job seekers alone. Besides, networks reveal only one aspect of the links that exist among individuals allowing access to information pertaining to the job market; the other crucial aspect of the links manifests itself in inter-household transfers of resources, both monetary and non-monetary.

Urban areas contribute to the rural standard of living by providing employment opportunities to the migrants from the rural areas and by enabling job holders to extend benefits and render help to their relatives and friends who did not migrate to the urban areas. Even among those who are natives and who do not have relatives in rural areas, the prevalence of transfers helps households to cope with risks (relating to employment, consumption, health, and shelter) and to reduce their vulnerability.

In this chapter our primary objective is to highlight the factors that determine the transfer of resources or the exchange of help among households/individuals. The organization of the chapter is as follows. In this section we review some of the studies relating to transfers and remittances. Sections 6.2 and 6.3 present the quantitative work based on our sample. The main findings are summarized in Section 6.4.

Often transfers across individuals are explained in terms of altruism, which means that $dT/dY<0$; where T stands for 'transfers' and Y for the recipient's income. As the recipient's income drops, under the conditions of altruism his relative/friend/co-villager is expected to extend him help. On the other hand, when transfers are motivated by the practice of exchange rather than altruism, transfers increase with the recipient's income, i.e. $dT/dY > 0$. This implies that as the recipient's income falls the donor realizes that the recipient's ability to reciprocate the donor's help also declines, and hence, the amount of contribution made by the donor tapers off. A lower expected value of reciprocation lowers the amount of the present transfer. But under the practice of 'strategic exchange', as Stark (1995) elaborates lucidly, the equation is $dT/dY<0$. If the donor feels that his help extended at the time of the need of his relative/friend/neighbour would enhance the gratification of the recipient, which ensures reciprocation in the future, then with a decline in the recipient's income, transfers tend to increase. But we may note that as we cross the boundaries of altruism and take recourse to the concept of 'strategic exchange' in explaining transfers, it would be quite unrealistic to presume a linear relationship between T and Y. In other words, it is less likely that the donor would continue to have the same expectations of receiving enhanced gratification from the recipient in the futrue, for all levels of decline in the latter's income. With a larger fall in the income of the recipient, particularly beyond a certain level, the donor may feel that the recipient would never be able to overcome his present crisis and reciprocate the contributions that the donor has made, and hence he may decide to reduce his contributions to the recipient. This would explain why friends contribute more when a needy person is only temporarily ill, and why they contribute less when the chances of his survival are reduced, though actually more contributions may be required in such situations of life threatening illnesses or accidents.

Till a certain point the donor may think that the recipient's gratitude would increase with transfers and hence reciprocation in the future would remain assured. But beyond a point the donor may realize that the enhanced gratification of the recipient need not be necessarily translated into material benefits that he expects in the future from the recipient of today. We call this non-linear strategic exchange. Symbolically

$$\frac{dT}{dY} < 0 \text{ if } Y \geq \overline{Y}$$

$$> 0 \text{ if } Y < \overline{Y}$$

where $\overline{Y}$, the critical level beyond which the donor's perception of his expectation being converted into material benefits in terms of reciprocation, undergoes a significant change.

All this, however, is not meant to suggest that individuals do not behave altruistically. As Lauby and Stark (1988) cite the example from the Philippines, young women, whose labour market earnings are less than that of their male counterparts, are still chosen as the family's migrant because parents find their daughters to be more altruistic than their sons. Similarly, in Indian society parents are often found to be living with one of their children whose income could possibly be substantially lower than his/her siblings; this fact may be explained in terms of altruism.

But it is important to note that mutual altruism does not necessarily result in social harmony. Both the donor and the recipient may end up being worse off in spite of the enhanced transfers prompted by an increase in altruism (Stark, 1995). In his earlier work, Stark (1989) argued that an economy with substantial levels of altruism will be Pareto superior to an economy with an absence of altruism, while an economy with a little altruism may be inferior to an economy with no altruism at all. This outcome arises from the fact that altruism can increase the possibilities for exploitation and limit the availability of credible strategies, thus narrowing the range of possible beneficial social arrangements. Hence, exploitation and strategic behaviour prompt commercialization, which is based on pure self-interest.

Stark (1995) takes a more realistic view of transfers, particularly the remittance behaviour of migrants, by imputing a strategic motive to it. He argues that migrants remit to non-migrants not because of altruistic considerations but instead they are guided by self-interest. The high-skilled workers who migrate to the urban areas want the low-skilled workers to stay back at the place of origin because their presence in the urban labour market could raise the supplies of labour, which in turn may reduce the ongoing wage rate. And this would mean a considerable fall in the earnings of the high-skilled workers as well. By remitting their earnings they are, therefore, able to protect their self-interest. In addition, the remittances to their homes encourage their relatives/friends to stay on in the rural areas instead of coming to urban areas in search of jobs for which they lack the requisite skills.

On the whole, it appears that though altruism as an attribute or a principle in life is an admirable virtue it does not always result in an improved situation. At times an increase in altruism can adversely affect both the donor and the recipient in spite of prompting enhanced rates of transfers. Hence, mutual altruism does not necessarily result in social harmony. This is because, as mentioned above, altruism can lead to exploitation and reduce the range of possible beneficial social arrangements. Altruism does not eliminate conflict and it can actually worsen the situation of all the parties involved in the exchange or transfer of assets, hence opening the way to exploitation and strategic behaviour. Thus individuals may prefer to adopt self-interested behaviour in the pursuit of commercialization.

Against the backdrop of this framework, if we recall the physical segmentation of the labour market and the prevailing practice of informal networks facilitating job accessibility, as explained in Chapters 1, 2, and 3, it will not be difficult to perceive the situation of surplus labour and a wage cut resulting from the subsequent migration of low-skilled relatives/friends of the high-skilled workers. Under such conditions remittances though prompted by self-interest still act as income-equalizing and welfare-increasing mechanisms by enhancing allocative efficiency.

The process of such strategic transfers comes to an end once the larger waves of migration of low-skilled workers from the rural areas to the urban areas take place. However, once the high-skilled workers are able to form their own groups and are able to carve an identity for themselves, their earnings remain unaffected by the inflow of low-skilled workers. Hence, remittances at that stage stop as the need to buy off the low-skilled workers disappears. In other words, the more organized the high-skilled workers are in forming groups and in protecting their wages, the less is their willingness to remit their earnings judged from the point of view of strategic behaviour. In the urban informal sector where such group formation is less likely to exist, remittances are expected to be higher, whereas in the organized sector where unions exist to protect the wages of workers, remittances may be expected to be low. This explanation helps us understand why unprotected workers with comparatively low earnings still continue to remit. Further, even if skill differences between migrant workers in the urban informal sector and their non-migrant relatives are not significant—both the groups, let us say, are unskilled—the migrants would still like to discourage and prevent their relatives from migrating as the possibility of wage reduction due to an influx of unskilled labour from the rural areas is much more threatening to their self-interest than an influx of skilled labour. Besides, the rising cost of providing food and shelter, and other expenses that the first comers are likely to incur for their relatives when they migrate, prompt the former to prefer the option of sending home remittances. However, not all these claims are empirically verifiable. In this chapter we only seek to examine if the practice of transfers—both monetary and non-monetary—is motivated by altruism or the principle of exchange (or strategic exchange).

6.2 Remittances/Help Received and Offered

Table 6.1 presents the savings profile of the slum households. A significant percentage of households seem to have savings in the bank (34 per cent), of which around 56 per cent have at least Rs. 1,000 in their accounts. However, the rate of informal savings, i.e. to retain money with one-self or with someone else in the family/community, is also not insignificant (around 37 per cent). Savings in the form of chit funds or with what is popularly known as committee are also practiced by the slum dwellers. In our sample 12 per cent of the households chose to have their savings in this form, of which around 66 per cent have at least Rs. 1,000.

The next question relates to the monetary transfers that take place across households and regions. Table 6.2 shows that around 84 per cent of the respondents sent remittances to their parents who

TABLE 6.1: TYPE OF SAVINGS

Type	% of HH with Savings	Proportion of HH with Savings More than Rs. 1,000 to total HH with Savings of all Amounts
Bank Savings	34.0	56.4
Self/Other	37.3	14.7
Post Office	2.9	43.5
Provident Funds	4.7	55.3
Insurance	6.1	69.4
Chit Funds/Committees	11.6	65.6
Fixed Deposits	5.7	78.3
Other	0.5	50.0
Loans Offered	11.7	78.7

TABLE 6.2: MONETARY TRANSFERS

	Remittances Sent to		Remittances Received from	
	Proportion of HH Responding 'Yes' to Total Respondents	Proportion of HH which Sent More Than Rs. 1,000 to Total No. of HH which Sent Money	Proportion of HH Responding 'Yes' to Total Respondents	Proportion of HH which Sent More Than Rs. 1,000 to Total No. of HH which Sent Money
Parents	84.4	51.9	60.9	57.1
Children	14.1	59.3	0.0	—
Siblings	7.5	50.0	13.6	66.7
Spouse's Relatives	1.6	50.0	18.2	50.0
Member of the Same Caste Group	0.4	0.0	4.5	100.0
Co-villagers	0.8	50.0	4.5	100.0
Others	0.8	50.0	9.1	50.0

Note: '—' stands for amount not indicated.

lived in the place of origin. Another 14 per cent remitted to their children who did not migrate with the principal earners, and 7.5 per cent transferred their earnings to their brothers/sisters. Spouse's relatives, members of the same caste group, and co-villagers do not account for a large percentage of households which send remittances. However, the fact that some of the households remit to both parents/ children, on the one hand, and, on the other, to relatives/friends is a matter of significance from the analytical point of view. In fact, many of the households which are found to remit have been sending more than Rs. 1,000, a figure taken to indicate the significance of the amount. More importantly, non-monetary transfers are quite evident which, like monetary transfers, flow both ways. Figures on both the help given and the help received would indicate close associations among the households (Table 6.3). Households which remit are largely found to own cultivable land and/or a house at the place of origin (Table 6.4). Also, most of them pay regular visits to the place of origin. All this suggests that remittances are not purely based on generosity or social practices. If we ignore the economic reasons behind remittances and transfers, a great deal of information will be lost which would help us understand some of the issues raised in the previous section of this chapter.

TABLE 6.3: NON-MONETARY TRANSFERS

	% of HH Responding 'Yes' in the Sample	
	Help Offered	Help Offered
Help 1	47.4	45.0
Help 2	35.8	31.7
Help 3	23.3	21.8

Notes: (1) Help includes the following categories: (a) gave food, (b) helped find a job, (c) helped with child care, (d) gave emotional support, encouragement, (e) provided shelter, (f) gave clothing, (g) helped find bridegroom, (h) helped with household work, (i) helped connect with people, (j) taught trade, (k) helped children get access to schools, and (l) others.

(2) Help (i), i = 1, 2, and 3 represent the major help offered/received, ranked in the order of importance.

TABLE 6.4: REMITTANCES AND CONTACTS

Remittances sent to	Among those Remitting		
	% of HH with Cultivable Land at the Place of Origin	% of HH with House at the Place of Origin	% of HH Visiting the Place of Origin
Parents	57.0	83.9	99.1
Children	70.4	92.6	96.3
Siblings	64.3	85.7	100.0
Spouse's Relatives	50.0	100.0	75.0
Members of the Same Caste Group	0.0	100.0	100.0
Co-villagers	50.0	50.0	50.0
Others	100.0	100.0	100.0

6.3 Modelling Decision to Remit or Help

Against the backdrop of the argument presented in Section 6.1 we examine the data collected in response to the following two questions:

(a) Did you send money to parents/children/brother or sister/spouse's relatives/members of the same caste group/co-villagers/others?

(b) Have you given any other kind of help to family/relatives at your place of origin?

These two questions were asked separately to the household head/principal earner in order to capture both the monetary and the non-monetary transfers. As the responses were recorded in terms of 'yes' and 'no', we estimate here a binomial logit model for both monetary and non-monetary transfers. The dependent variables for the two sets of regression are remittances sent (REMS) and help given (HELPG), each taking a value of 0 and 1 for responses 'no' and 'yes' respectively. Variables that are taken to explain the responses are household size (HHSZ), a dummy making a distinction between illiterate household head (EDUC=0) and those who are literate and/or educated (EDUC=1), and duration of migration (DMIG) in terms of the number of years, with a value of 0 for non-migrants or those born in Delhi. Their response to the question whether they put aside any money in the form of savings is again represented in terms of a dummy (SAVED, 0 for no savings and 1 for a positive response). This variable is taken to represent the migrant worker's ability to offer (monetary) assistance to others.

If the household has a plot of cultivable land or a house at the place of origin or if the members of the household keep visiting the place of origin, the migrant worker's association with other members of the household/co-villagers/friends is expected to be stronger, this we captured in terms of a dummy called CONTD. It takes a value of 1 if any of the characteristics mentioned above is present, otherwise 0. The ownershiop of property or contacts at the place of origin are likely to increase the rate and amount of transfers.

If the household head ever received any monetary or non-monetary assistance from anyone other than those with whom he lives under the same roof, he is expected to respond positively to the question whether he sent any money or offered any help to others. Keeping in view the sense of reciprocation, REMR and HELPR are taken to represent the remittances received and the help received respectively. Income of the household head (HHINC) and the nature of employment are taken interchangeably to capture the effect of the ability to remit. Though the household might be putting aside money in the form of savings, low or irregular incomes may not enable one to send remittances. As there are three categories of employment—casual employment, self-employment, and regular-wage salaried employment—we have taken two dummies for self-employment (SELF) and regular-wage employment (RSAL).

As mentioned above, two sets of regressions have been estimated corresponding to monetary and non-monetary assistance. The results of the binomial logit model (with marginal effects) are reported in Tables 6.5 and 6.6 respectively.

Empirical results show that with household size the probability of sending monetary remittances declines. Literates are more likely to remit as compared to illiterates. It is interesting to note that if the household head received any remittance he is less likely to reciprocate in monetary terms. But the coefficient of REMR is not highly significant

TABLE 6.5: REGRESSION RESULTS: MONETARY TRANSFERS (MODEL: BINOMIAL LOGIT) *DEP. VAR: REMS*

Indep. Variables	Equ. 1		Equ. 2	
	Coefficients	Marginal Effects	Coefficients	Marginal Effects
HHSZ	-0.35 (-6.6)*	-0.06	-0.33 (-6.94)*	-0.06
EDU	0.28 (2.0)*	0.05	0.28 (2.03)*	0.05
DMIG	0.12 (2.96)*	0.02	0.12 (3.08)*	0.02
SAVED	0.04 (0.35)	0.01	0.02 (0.18)	0.004
CONTD	2.68 (5.1)*	0.48	2.69 (5.13)*	0.48
REMR	-0.93 (-1.73)**	-0.17	-1.04 (-1.9)**	-0.19
HELPR	0.93 (5.25)*	0.17	0.93 (5.23)*	0.17
HHINC			0.0001 (2.78)*	0.00002
SELF	0.23 (1.1)	0.04		
RSAL	-0.02 (-0.73)	-0.003		
INTER	-2.92 (-4.76)*	-0.52	-3.06 (-5.00)*	-0.55
Chi-square	192.78		199.38	
N	802		802	

Note: Figures in parentheses are t-ratios. The asterisk marks *, **, *** are significant at 5, 10, 20 per cent levels, respectively. Chi-square values are significant at the 1 per cent level.

TABLE 6.6: REGRESSION RESULTS: NON-MONETARY TRANSFERS (MODEL: BINOMIAL LOGIT) *DEP. VAR: HELPG*

Indep. Variables	Equ. 1		Equ. 2	
	Coefficients	Marginal Effects	Coefficients	Marginal Effects
HHSZ	-0.03 (-0.44)	-0.007	-0.04 (-6.63)*	-0.01
EDU	0.48 (1.83)*	0.11	0.44 (1.70)**	0.01
DMIG	0.07 (1.32)***	0.015	0.06 (1.2)	0.01
SAVED	0.92 (3.28)	0.2	0.85 (3.03)*	0.19
CONTD	0.93 (2.57)*	0.2	0.95 (2.61)*	0.21
REMR	-0.19 (-0.23)**	-0.04	-0.27 (-0.32)**	-0.06
HELPR	4.49 (16.8)*	0.99	4.48 (16.87)*	1.00
HHINC			0.00003 (0.71)	0.00001
SELF	-0.43 -(1.42)***	-0.09		
RSAL	-0.003 (-0.01)	-0.0007		
INTER	-3.84 (-6.30)*	-0.84	-3.91 (-6.52)*	-0.87
Chi-square	646.03		644.0	
N	802		802	

Note: Same as Table 6.5.

at the 5 per cent level. On the other hand, if the household received any help (non-monetary) the probability of sending remittances increases. We may note here that while we address the issue of reciprocation in this manner, the results need to be interpreted carefully. This is because remittances or help received from and remittances or help given to persons or households need not be the same; and it is not possible to figure out the mapping from the questionnaire.

The longer the duration of migration the more the probability of sending remittances. This is understandable because short-duration migrants are more prone to risk in the job market compared to the long-duration migrants. The longer the stay in the urban areas, the more the migrants manage to experience upward occupational/income mobility and stability in earnings and hence they remit part of their earnings. Their response to the question whether they saved any money does not turn out to be significant. The contact dummy representing cultivable land at home at or regular visits to the place of origin is highly significant, with a positive coefficient. The dummies taken to capture the differences in the nature of employment are not statistically significant. However, when the nature of employment dummies are replaced by the dummy for income of the head of the household, it turns out to be positively significant, confirming that with an increase in income the probability of sending remittances increases.

In the equation for help given (non-monetary assistance), more or less the same variables turn out to be significant with signs, as mentioned above. Help given is highly influenced by help received, the t-ratio being around 16.8. The dummy representing the response to savings takes a positive coefficient, which is statistically significant. However, neither the nature of employment nor the income variable turns out to be significant in influencing the probability to extend help.

On the whole, the results are suggestive of certain prevailing practices of sending remittances, which seem to be influenced by a strong sense of reciprocation, the capability of the remitter, his (her) level of education, and the job market instability that s(he) faces. Large household size implying a large dependency ratio, lowers the probability of giving monetary or non-monetary assistance.

It is, however, difficult to judge from these findings whether remittances or help given are based purely on altruism or exchange. But empirical findings tend to extend support in favour of the exchange hypothesis, as the practice of reciprocation seems to be quite strong. The fact that help received influences positively the decision to remit or extend help is indicative of this tendency. On the other hand, the negative coefficient of the dummy representing remittances received in the equation for remittances sent and its pure insignificance in the equation for help given are indicative of a different tendency, which could be either altruism or strategic exchange. But the latter seems to have a greater possibility if it is rationalized in the light of the positive coefficient of help received in all equations. Feelings of exchange and strategic exchange, as suggested in Section 6.1, are closer to each other than the feelings of exchange and altruism from an individual point of view.

6.4 Conclusion

In this chapter we made an attempt to assess the purpose of monetary and/or non-monetary transfers that take place among the slum dwellers in Delhi. Notwithstanding the limitations of the data, it is quite clear that monetary/non-monetary help given depends on the help received from others. In other words, it is based on a sense of reciprocation. Hence, interpreting remittances or transfers purely on the basis of the feeling of altruism may not be correct. However, while suggesting that the principle of exchange is in practice, it must be admitted that our analysis could not identify if the recipients of help/transfers were the same as those who had extended such help/transfers in the past to the present donors.

Other factors which matter in determining transfers are also identified. Education, caste, household size, ability to save, contact with the place of origin, and the duration of migration are some of the determinants of remittances and/or help given. That property at or visits to the place of origin influence the decision to remit is again indicative of the practice of exchange, though on its face value altruism seems to be the motivating factor. With an increase in the duration of migration people tend to remit more because both their ability to earn and to save increases over time and with experience in the urbon labour market. However, with an increase in experience in the urban labour market, their ability to help others in accessing jobs also increases, and hence more relatives and co-villagers are expected to migrate to the city. As this may adversely affect their future in the urban labour market due to an increase in supplies of labour, and also increase their liabilities on the domestic front if they were to put up the newcomers in their own households, remittances are considered to be better substitutes. On the whole, the issue of remittances needs to be viewed in the light of self-interest-based behaviour. The practices of networks in the job market, analysed in the earlier chapters, are also indicative of the practice of mutual help, that is, the principle of exchange rather than pure altruism. These findings have important policy implications. The prevailing practices of informal mechnisms of exchange can provide a strong basis to the supportive role of the government in the context of poverty reduction and slum improvement.

CHAPTER 7

WOMEN IN THE URBAN INFORMAL SECTOR

7.1 Introduction

A large majority of Indian women who perform a great deal of unpaid work within the household, which falls outside the market economy, are often forced by economic necessity, particularly in the urban areas, to combine domestic work with other remunerative jobs in the informal sector. Within this sector there exist opportunities to work on a part-time basis, procure contracts for home-based activities and piece-rate jobs, and to exploit the overall flexibility to combine household activities with income-yielding jobs to suit their convenience. The lack of entry barriers, moderate skill requirements in terms of formal education (from the employees' point of view), and the scope to avoid meeting the requirements of labour laws (from the employers' point of view) encourage the growth of activities in the urban informal sector. In self-employed or own-account enterprises, flexibility in working hours is enormous, though the contribution of women labour to value-added tends to be largely underestimated. Even when they are employed as wage labour, their contribution to family income is considered to be marginal as their acceptance of income-yielding jobs is only residual to fulfilling family responsibilities to which no economic value is usually ascribed, implying their opportunity cost to be zero.

While examining the issue of women in the urban informal sector, we may recall the two arguments offered in Chapter 3 relating to the physical segmentation of the labour market and the role of informal networks in providing information on jobs. Though segmentation along the lines of caste, skill, and education has drawn the attention of scholars in the past, the physical segmentation of the labour market is a relatively under-researched area. By physical segmentation we mean, as defined earlier, the inaccessibility of certain kinds of jobs by certain groups of individuals, primarily because of the distances within a city. Hence, occupational choice, particularly that of women, is largely determined by the narrow choice or range of jobs available within the geographic area where they reside rather than by what they are actually capable of pursuing. Particularly for women in low-income households, contact-based jobs are crucial as home-based activities, piece-rate, and contractual jobs, which they usually prefer, are accessible only through acquaintances and friends. Being a relative/friend of an already employed person is an advantage or asset for the potential job seeker. However, such a contact-based job search ends up in providing jobs only in neighbourhoods close to their residence, as the early settlers, who help their relatives, friends, members of the same caste groups, and co-villagers by providing information on the available job and the living space, are usually engaged in similar activities in the vicinity.

As mentioned in Chapter 3 the willingness to reside near the work place is determined by many factors, some of which could be traced to the very nature of the activities that workers, particularly women, perform. The self-employed workers in petty manufacturing and repairing activities often have their enterprises within the household premises. Similarly, the self-employed and the wage labourers in trading activities are required to use their work place for residential purposes as well from the security point of view. Another reason to stay in the vicinity can be identified in terms of multi-jobs that the members of the low-income households usually take up. Women who combine their household activities with jobs outside the home are often engaged in similar kinds of jobs but in a large number of households (for instance, domestic maids), and hence they prefer to have the place of work and the place of residence close to each other. Even if the total income earned from all jobs closer to the place of residence is less than the income which could have been earned from a job available at a distant place, this first option would be preferred as long as the cost of commuting and the opportunity cost of the time spent on commuting are large enough to lower the potential earnings than the actual earnings. The preference or desire to reside in the neighbourhood of relatives and friends or co-villagers may be traced to economic, sociological, and political factors, as mentioned in Chapters 2 and 3.

The organization of the chapter is as follows. Section 7.2 briefly reviews some of the recent studies on similar themes. Section 7.3 examines the data and delineates broad patterns pertaining to women's employment in the informal sector. Econometric analysis is carried out in Section 7.4, and the major findings are summarized in Section 7.5.

7.2 Review of Studies

Though it is difficult to arrive at a comprehensive definition and estimate of employment in the urban informal sector, some previous studies have attempted to estimate its share (for a detailed review see Mitra, 1994). In non-agricultural activities (both rural and urban combined), the relative size of the informal sector, estimated on the basis of the assumption that small establishments and own-account enterprises fall into the so-called informal sector, turned out to be around 61 per cent and 72 per cent in 1990 as per the Economic Census data and the data provided by DGET, Ministry of Labour respectively (Mitra, 2001a).

Presuming that all organized sector activities are conducted in the urban areas, the estimate of urban unorganized/informal sector employment has been derived for several time points, from 1983 to 1997. Although the figures are not comparable in a strict sense, as large and small samples of the NSS may yield dissimilar results, they are indicative of a rise in low-productivity jobs in the urban economy during the 1990s (Mitra, 2001b). Besides, contractual employment and piece-rate jobs within the organized sector, which are not necessarily reflected in the figures on organized sector employment, are also on the rise (Mitra, 2000). Further, as the critics of the new development strategy hold, the organized industrial growth rate may not be high in the long run and the present low rate of infrastructural investment would slow down even the rate of agricultural growth, leading to larger inflows of rural migrant labour to urban areas and to the subsequent expansion of the informal sector (see Kundu, 1997). The limited spread of the organized industry and the adoption of capital-intensive technology lead to a residual absorption of labour in the urban informal sector. Further, women in general suffer from two sets of discrimination in the labour markets: (a) pre-market discrimination involving lack of access to estimation, training, experience—factors which increase human capital and enhance the marginal product of labour, and (b) post-market discrimination involving differential wages for a similar quantum of human capital. These constraints imply that a large proportion of the women job seekers end up working in the informal sector which does not require much education or skill (National Institute of Urban Affairs, 1991).

Women's participation in the labour market, particularly in the informal sector, was expected to increase in the post-reform period partly as a substitution of cheaper female labour for male labour and partly due to economic distress resulting from a lower rate of employment of male members in their households (Deshpande, 2001). Based on a survey of slum women in Mumbai, Deshpande (2001) confirms that as they entered the labour market they preferred to be engaged in occupations where the nature of work was more or less an extension of the work they carried out as housewives. Such occupations allowed them to carry out their economic work along with their domestic work. 'In other words, these women entered the informal sector of Mumbai's economy, either as self-employed or as contract workers or as wage workers, mainly because there was flexibility in the working hours' (Deshpande, 2001, p. 337).

The survey results also revealed that the work place of most women was within walking distance from their residence; in fact, many of them had compromised and accepted lower wages compared to those offered in their first job, as the current job provided security and the work place was located close to their residence. Based on a case study of sales women in Ernakulam, Patrick (2001) confirms that women workers face both occupational segregation and wage discrimination in the labour market. Besides, about 32 per cent of their average salary or 16 per cent of the total household income which they account for in terms of their activities as housewives—estimated on the basis of the opportunity cost of time approach—remains mostly unrecognized.

Mukhopadhyay (1999) estimates that female employment in the urban unorganized sector increased from 12.71 to 15.11 million over the period 1983 to 1987–8. She wrote that within unorganized manufacturing the female intensity is high in own-account manufacturing enterprises, which run presumably at low-earnings and low-productivity levels. Besides, a large number of them seem to be employed on a part-time basis in both non-directory manufacturing establishments and own-account manufacturing enterprises. Women are being absorbed in large numbers in hired-wage work which means that they are being hired only on a part-time basis, suggesting that even within the informal sector women workers get a bad deal (Mukhopadhyay, 1999; Institute of Social Studies Trust, 1997; Kalpagam, 2001). Kalpagam notes that women's absorption in certain export industries such as garments, jewellery, and electronics, has been high but it is mostly based on contractual employment, and second, the nature of work and the working conditions are far below the tolerable limits.

The study on women in the informal sector carried out by the National Institute of Urban Affairs (1991) in 6 Indian cities argues that women in this sector suffer from a dual disadvantage, which manifests itself first, in the lopsided division of labour, and second, the placing of the majority of poor women at the bottom of the income scale across various activities. They are employed mainly in jobs at the lower rungs of the income scale. The levels of monetary return are generally low in the informal sector and are particularly low in the case of women workers. Even in the same activity the earnings of female workers are lower than those of their male counterparts. This is either because women perform less skilled jobs or because they are considered to be less productive. While examining occupational mobility, that is, vertical mobility, which means improvement in monetary returns and social status either as a result of a shift to a better regarded and more highly paid economic activity or promotion and expansion in the same activity, the study noted its marginal presence in the case of women in the informal sector. Only about 14 per cent of 1,200 respondents changed their main economic activity in the past five years. Moreover, in conventional caste-based economic activities occupational mobility was totally absent. Keeping in view some of these issues, we attempt in this chapter to delineate patterns relating to the employment of women from the slum households in Delhi.

7.3 Data Analysis

Before presenting in the next section the econometric analysis of the choice of occupation/employment category, we examine here certain economic and demographic characteristics of the women workers from the slum households in Delhi.

Quite contrary to the popular expectation that an increasing number of girl children is employed in the informal sector, it is noted that only 2 per cent of the total women workers belong to the age group 0–14 (see Table 7.1). This could be mainly because girls join the labour market only as helpers to their mothers, and hence their explicit participation is unlikely to get recorded. Similarly, not a

TABLE 7.1: PERCENTAGE DISTRIBUTION OF WOMEN WORKERS BY AGE, HOUSEHOLD SIZE AND DURATION OF MIGRATION

Age Group	% Dist. of Women Workers	HH Size	% Dist. of Women Workers
0–14	2.2	1	0.4
15–20	13.3	2	6.9
21–30	29.6	3	9.0
31–40	35.2	4	17.2
41–55	13.7	5	26.2
55 and above	6.0	6	18.0
Total	100.0	7 and above	22.3

Duration of Migration	% Dist. of Women Workers
Non-migrants	30.9
Up to 1 year	0.4
2 to 3 years	3.0
4 to 5 years	1.7
6 to 7 years	3.9
8 to 10 years	5.1
11 to 15 years	15.9
15 years and above	39.1
Total	100.0

very significant proportion of workers is found in the age bracket 55 and above, which is possibly because of the unavailability of jobs for older persons. Employment opportunities in the informal sector do not exist uniformly across the board for individuals in all age groups. Jobs based on physical exertion, enterprises using complex and mechanized technology, and even domestic services show a strong preference for workers who are physically fit and who are likely to be less absent from work. Around 65 per cent of the women workers fall into the age group 21 to 40. However, we may note that if older women are found largely in contractual jobs, that too not on a regular basis, under-reporting tends to be considerably high.

With an increase in household size, participation of women in the labour market seems to increase. As evident from Table 7.1, households with 5 members and households with 7 members and above account for around 26 and 22 per cent respectively of the total women workers in the slums.

This is indicative of the fact that women labour is treated as a reservoir and released only under economic compulsions. Hence, women from large households are more vulnerable as they need to shoulder greater responsibilities within their own households and at the same time they need to participate in the labour market to add to the household income.

It is interesting to note that a large majority of women workers are either non-migrants or migrants who have been residing in the city for a very long time (more than 15 years). Short and medium duration migrant households are less likely to have their women members employed in the labour market. This pattern is an outcome of both economic and social factors: women's work participation is closely associated with their residence in the city; short and medium duration migrants are possibly restricted by their social and cultural ethos which prevents their explicit participation in the labour market. Alternately, women members of these households are perhaps faced with more demanding domestic duties as required during the process of settling down in the city and hence they are not available for long hours of work outside the home, while the male members keep struggling to acquire the work opportunities of their choice.

The employment structure of females appears to be very different from that of males. While male workers are more or less evenly distributed across the three employment categories/casual employment, regular-wage/salaried employment, and self-employment—a large majority of the women workers (more than 70 per cent) are engaged in casual employment (Table 7.2). This could be, as mentioned above, due to the flexibility that such jobs offer in terms of working hours, lack of barriers to entry, and the skill requirements.

The percentage distribution of workers across occupation types also reveals considerable gender differentials. These occupation groups have been formed, as mentioned in Chapter 3, on the basis of the detailed listing of economic activities that workers reported during the survey. More than 56 per cent of the women workers are employed in personal services. Manufacturing and commercial services account for another 20 per cent. Though an almost equal proportion of male workers is also employed in manufacturing and commercial services, differences persist in relation to other activities. Construction accounts for the largest share of male workers (26.6 per cent).

The detailed description of activities, based on which the occupation groups has been prepared, is indicative of the fact that workers from slum households are mostly engaged in the informal sector (see

TABLE 7.2: PERCENTAGE DISTRIBUTION OF WORKERS BY EMPLOYMENT CATEGORY/OCCUPATION TYPE, AND AVERAGE MONTHLY INCOME

Category of Employment	Male Workers %	Female Workers (%)	Average Income in Rs. (Male)	Average income in Rs. (Female)
Casual Employment	36.3	71.7	2597.4 (59.5)	1359.7 (88.5)
Regular-Wage/ Salaried	32.9	14.6	2163.9 (64.0)	1357.4 (42.1)
Self-Employment	30.8	13.7	2619.6 (90.6)	1582.5 (50.3)
Total	100	100		
Occupation Type				
Professional	6.0	3.4	2873.8 (66.6)	2250.0 (43.3)
Sales	14.7	4.3	2110.05 (58.5)	1295.0 (65.0)
Trade	16.6	6.4	2767.2 (101.3)	1616.1 (51.3)
Personal Service	3.7	56.2	1955.3 (126.3)	952.1 (48.4)
Manufacturing	9.6	8.2	2201.8 (79.2)	1745.8 (79.7)
Commercial Service	10.7	11.2	3441.3 (62.8)	2862.4 (65.7)
Transport	3.8	0.4	2653.8 (41.0)	2750.0 (0.0)
Tailoring, Knitting, etc.	2.9	1.7	2472.5 (52.7)	1200.0 (58.1)
Construction	26.6	7.3	2127.9 (36.4)	1466.2 (31.9)
Security	1.0	0.0	2254.8 (28.8)	—
Repairing	4.5	0.8	2381.9 (54.8)	2000.0 (70.7)
Total	100	100		

Note: Figures in parentheses give the coefficient of the variations.

note at the end of Chapter 3).[1] The cross-classification of women workers by employment categories and occupation groups also substantiates the claim that a large majority of them are either in casual employment or self-employment which by definition mostly fall into the informal sector, though casual employment in the organized sector can also exist (Table 7.3). Even among those who are listed as professionals not a single woman is found to be in regular-wage/salaried employment. Occupation groups such as trade and tailoring, etc., are dominated by self-employed workers, though tailoring, etc., also offer regular-wage jobs (25 per cent). Construction and manufacturing seem to comprise a great deal of regular-wage jobs; around 88 and 37 per cent respectively of the total employment in these occupations account for regular-wage/salaried jobs.

Substantiating further with evidence the vulnerability of women workers from slum households, Table 7.4 shows that around 65 per cent are illiterate. Only 3 per cent of them acquired education above the secondary level. An overwhelming proportion of illiterate women workers is engaged in personal services (56.6 per cent). Only among those with an education of above the secondary level, 57 per cent are

TABLE 7.3: CROSS-CLASSIFICATION OF WOMEN WORKERS BY CATEGORY OF EMPLOYMENT AND OCCUPATION TYPE

Occupation Type	Category of Employment		
	Casual Employment	Regular-Wage/ Salaried	Self-Employment
Professional	62.5	0.0	37.5
Sales	30.0	30.0	40.0
Trade	13.3	0.0	86.7
Personal Service	91.6	6.1	2.3
Manufacturing	42.1	36.8	21.1
Commercial Service	100.0	0.0	0.0
Transport	0.0	0.0	100.0
Tailoring, Knitting, etc.	0.0	25.0	75.0
Construction	11.8	88.2	0.0
Security	—	—	—
Repairing	50.0	0.0	50.0
Total	71.7	14.6	13.7

Note: Each row adds up to 100 per cent. No woman is found employed as a security worker.

TABLE 7.4: WOMEN WORKERS BY OCCUPATION AND EDUCATION

(*in %*)

Occupation Type	Illiterate	Literate with No Formal Schooling	Class 1 to 5	Class 6 to Secondary	Above Secondary
Professional	0.0	0.0	3.2	8.8	57.1
Sales	5.9	0.0	0.0	2.9	0.0
Trade	5.9	0.0	16.1	2.9	0.0
Personal Service	56.6	55.5	64.5	52.9	28.6
Manufacturing	7.2	0.0	9.7	14.7	0.0
Commercial Service	13.2	11.1	3.2	11.8	0.0
Transport	0.7	0.0	0.0	0.0	0.0
Tailoring, Knitting, etc.	1.3	11.1	3.2	0.0	0.0
Construction	9.2	11.1	0.0	2.9	14.3
Security	—	—	—	—	—
Repairing	0.0	11.1	0.0	2.9	0.0
Total	100	100	100	100	100
	(65.2)	(3.9)	(13.3)	(14.6)	(3.0)

Note: Each column adds up to 100 per cent. Figures in parentheses add up to 100 per cent across the row.

found as professionals. Otherwise, in the rest of the categories more than at least half of the workers are in personal services. However, those with formal schooling are possibly located in the upper strata of the same occupation class. In other words, the heterogeneity even within a particular occupation group needs to be acknowledged. The coefficient of variation of occupation-specific income shown within the parentheses in Table 7.2 highlights this point. In some of the occupations the coefficient of variation of income for women workers is even larger than that for male workers. Though women show a smaller variation in income in personal services it is not entirely negligible.

Returning to the question of the duration of migration, it is indeed interesting to note from Table 7.5 that only non-migrants and the long duration migrants (with more than 10 years of duration of residence) are employed in the better paying occupations such as the professionals. Not a single woman among those who had been residing in Delhi for the last 10 years or less is found in the professional occupations. Similarly, in sales, manufacturing, and commercial services short and medium duration migrants are thinly present. Only in personal services do migrants of all durations seem

TABLE 7.5: DISTRIBUTION OF WOMEN WORKERS BY MIGRATION STATUS AND OCCUPATION

Occupation Type	Duration of Migration								Total
	Non-Mig.	Up to 1 year	2–3 years	4–5 years	6–7 years	8–10 years	11–15 years	Above 15 years	
Professional	62.5	0.0	0.0	0.0	0.0	0.0	25.0	12.5	100.0
Sales	30.0	0.0	0.0	0.0	10.0	20.0	20.0	20.0	100.0
Trade	13.3	0.0	6.7	0.0	6.7	6.7	33.3	33.3	100.0
Personal Service	32.1	0.8	3.1	1.5	4.6	4.6	14.5	38.9	100.0
Manufacturing	15.8	0.0	5.3	0.0	0.0	0.0	26.3	52.6	100.0
Commercial Service	42.3	0.0	0.0	0.0	3.8	3.8	0.0	50.0	100.0
Transport	100.0	0.0	0.0	0.0	0.0	0.0	0.0	0.0	100.0
Tailoring, Knitting, etc.	0.0	0.0	0.0	25.0	0.0	0.0	50.0	25.0	100.0
Construction	23.5	0.0	5.9	5.9	0.0	11.8	11.8	41.2	100.0
Security	—	—	—	—	—	—	—	—	100.0
Repairing	50.0	0.0	0.0	0.0	0.0	0.0	0.0	50.0	100.0
Total	30.9	0.4	3.0	1.7	3.9	5.1	15.9	39.1	100.0

Note: Each row adds up to 100 per cent.

to be working. Two inferences can be drawn from this observation. As soon as women arrive in the city, occupations with lower skill requirements tend to absorb them in case they decide to join the labour market. On the other hand, those who join the labour market later after overcoming the initial hurdles of city life tend to locate in better paying jobs, possibly by operating through networks.

In Tables 7.6 and 7.7 the cross-classification of women workers as per various income classes and employment categories/occupations is given. A large number of casual workers (around 40 per cent) fall into the income class Rs. 501–1,000 per month. The poverty line for Delhi for the year 1999-2000 is estimated at Rs. 570 per month in terms of monthly per capita consumption expenditure.[2] That the minimum consumption expenditure per capita falls into the income class which accounts for a large percentage of casual women workers is indicative of their vulnerability in the labour market. Table 7.2 reveals that the average income of women workers in casual employment was almost half of the average income of male workers. Second, the average income of women in regular-wage/salaried employment is as low as that of casual women workers, though a larger percentage of women in regular wage jobs (35 per cent) are found in a slightly higher income class (Rs. 1,001–1,500), as com-

TABLE 7.6: DISTRIBUTION OF WOMEN WORKERS BY INCOME CLASSES AND EMPLOYMENT CATEGORIES

Income Class	Employment Category			Total
	Casual Employment	Regular-Wage/ Salaried Employment	Self-Employment	
0–300	3.6	0.0	0.0	2.6
301–500	14.4	5.9	9.4	12.5
501–1000	40.1	29.4	18.8	35.6
1001–1500	22.2	35.3	21.8	24.0
1501–2500	8.4	29.4	31.3	14.6
2501–4000	6.0	0.0	12.4	6.0
4001 and above	5.4	0.0	6.3	4.7
Total	100.0	100	100	100
	(71.7)	(14.6)	(13.7)	

Note: Each column adds up to 100 per cent. Figures in parentheses across the last row add up to 100 per cent.

TABLE 7.7: PERCENTAGE DISTRIBUTION OF WOMEN WORKERS BY OCCUPATION TYPES AND INCOME CLASSES

Occupation Type	Income Class							Total
	0–300	301–500	501–1,000	1,001–1,500	1,501–2,500	2,501–4,000	4,001 and above	
Professional	0.0	0.0	12.5	12.5	50.0	25.0	0.0	100.0 (3.4)
Sales	0.0	20.0	30.0	20.0	20.0	10.0	0.0	100.0 (4.3)
Trade	0.0	0.0	26.7	33.3	20.0	13.3	6.7	100.0 (6.4)
Personal Service	2.3	19.1	46.6	26.7	3.8	1.5	0.0	100.0 (56.2)
Manufacturing	5.3	5.3	26.3	10.5	36.8	5.3	10.5	100.0 (8.2)
Commercial Service	7.7	0.0	15.4	11.5	19.2	15.4	30.8	100.0 (11.2)
Transport	0.0	0.0	0.0	0.0	0.0	100.0	0.0	100.0 (0.4)
Tailoring, Knitting, etc.	0.0	25.0	25.0	25.0	25.0	0.0	0.0	100.0 (1.7)
Construction	0.0	0.0	17.6	41.2	41.2	0.0	0.0	100.0 (7.3)
Security	—	—	—	—	—	—	—	—
Repairing	0.0	0.0	50.0	0.0	0.0	50.0	0.0	100.0 (0.9)
Total	2.6	12.4	35.6	24.0	14.6	6.0	4.7	100.0

Note: Each row adds up to 100 per cent. Figures in parentheses in the last column add up to 100 per cent.

pared to casual workers (22 per cent). Women in self-employment earn the highest income though it is still much lower than the average income of males in the comparable category (Table 7.2). As Table 7.5 shows, around half of the self-employed women earn more than Rs. 1,500 per month.

Occupation-wise, it is again noted from Table 7.7 that more than 46 per cent women in personal services belong to the income class Rs. 501–1,000 and more than 20 per cent earn even less than that. In manufacturing and construction the largest shares (37 and 41 per cent respectively) correspond to a higher income class (Rs. 1,501–2,500 per month). In commercial services more than 30 per cent of the women workers earn at least Rs. 4,000 a month. Even in trade 33 per cent are in the income class Rs. 1,001–1,500 though their presence in the income class Rs. 501–1,000 is not negligible either (27 per cent). Quite compatible with these patterns, the highest average income is reported for women workers in commercial services (see Table 7.2) and the male-female wage gap is also quite low—the female average income being around 87 per cent of the male average income. In personal services, not only do women earn the lowest average income but even their remuneration is less than 50 per cent that of males (Table 7.2).

Distributing all women (both workers and non-workers) across various per capita expenditure size classes, we, however, note very different patterns as compared to their distribution across income classes. Table 7.8 shows that only 18 per cent of women in personal services incur a monthly per capita expenditure of Rs. 625 or less, though nearly 70 per cent earned an income of less than Rs. 1,000 per month, as noted above. This suggests that women workers engaged in personal services usually belong to households where male members are employed in high-income jobs, relatively speaking; hence their expenditure per capita tends to improve. On the other hand, in trade and sales around 20 and 30 per cent of the women workers incur an expenditure of less than Rs. 450 per month, which is even lower than the poverty line. Even in construction the percentage of women workers with a per capita expenditure of less than Rs. 450 per month is nearly 12 per cent, as high as that among non-workers, though none of the women construction workers earned an income of less than Rs. 500 a month. This reveals the fact that intra-household mobility of resources is not just one-way round, i.e. from males to females. Rather, women workers notwithstanding, their generally

TABLE 7.8: PERCENTAGE OF ALL WOMEN BY PER CAPITA EXPENDITURE SIZE CLASSES AND OCCUPATION TYPE (INCLUDING NON-WORKERS)

Occupation Type	Per Capita Expenditure Size Clases (Rs.)							Total
	Less than 275	275–449.99	450–624.99	625–799.99	800–974.99	975–1,149.99	1,150 and above	
Non-Workers	1.1	10.5	22.5	24.1	14.5	13.0	14.2	100.0
Professional	0.0	0.0	12.5	0.0	0.0	12.5	75.0	100.0
Sales	10.0	20.0	20.0	20.0	10.0	10.0	10.0	100.0
Trade	0.0	20.0	6.7	13.3	20.0	20.0	20.0	100.0
Personal Service	0.8	6.9	10.7	29.0	16.8	16.0	19.8	100.0
Manufacturing	0.0	0.0	36.8	31.6	10.5	0.0	21.1	100.0
Commercial Service	3.8	3.8	34.6	11.5	15.4	19.2	11.5	100.0
Transport	0.0	0.0	100.0	0.0	0.0	0.0	0.0	100.0
Tailoring,* Knitting, etc.	0.0	0.0	50.0	25.0	0.0	25.0	0.0	100.0
Construction	0.0	11.8	11.8	35.3	11.8	17.6	11.7	100.0
Security	—	—	—	—	—	—	—	100.0
Repairing	—	—	—	—	—	50.0	50.0	100.0
Total	1.2	10.1	21.8	24.2	14.6	13.3	14.8	100.0

Note: Every row adds up to 100 per cent.

low earnings compensate for others within the household by sacrificing their own income towards the consumption expenditure for others. In the process many of them lead a below-the-poverty-line standard of living; this fact becomes much more evident particularly if we interpret the figures in the context of intra-household inequality of consumption, to which several studies have already offered empirical support (Agarwal, 1994; Miller, 1981; Moser, 1989; Standing, 1991). Besides, it is to be remembered that sacrifices of similar amounts are not the same for an individual in a high-income job and for another in a low-income job, at least from the economic point of view. Hence, mobility of resources in households from male workers (in relatively high-income categories) to the rest and that in households from female workers (in relatively low-income categories) to the rest have different implications not only in terms of female health, morbidity, and current income but also in terms of their ability to work in the long run and to enhance their future earnings.

In some of the middle- and higher-expenditure size classes a large proportion of the total women (around 40 per cent or so) belong to households with size being dominated by females, i.e. at least 60 per cent of the total household members are females (see Table 7.9). However, in lower expenditure size classes this is not the case. It may be inferred, therefore, that households with a larger number of females manage to augment their consumption expenditure per capita by accepting piece-rate jobs and other marginal work, which need not necessarily be registered in a survey as of this, due to the lack of continuity of such activities. This is in sharp contrast to the popular view which regards women members of the households as purely dependents. At least in the lower rungs of the society this does not seem to be the case; even the so-called dependents add considerably to the family income, although their contribution may be through petty or marginal jobs. And since such jobs are not carried out on a regular basis or in a significant way they often do not even get registered.

7.4 Occupational Choice: Econometric Analysis

In this section we examine the issue of occupational selection. We noted that even within the informal sector there could be a large range of activities, some of which may (or may not) be strongly preferable to women workers depending upon the location of the

TABLE 7.9: DISTRIBUTION OF ALL WOMEN BY PER CAPITA EXPENDITURE SIZE CLASSES AND THE NUMBER OF WOMEN PER HOUSEHOLD

Per Capita Exp. Size Class	Proportion of Women to total Household Members (%)							
	11–20	21–30	31–40	41–50	51–60	61–70	71–80	81–100
Less than 275	0.0	0.0	33.3	23.8	42.9	0.0	0.0	0.0
275–449.99	1.1	3.8	19.0	25.5	10.9	29.3	7.1	3.3
450–624.99	1.8	3.3	18.9	33.8	9.6	20.6	9.3	2.8
625–799.79	2.3	3.4	20.2	29.3	6.4	28.4	7.7	2.3
800–974.99	5.3	5.3	25.3	24.2	4.5	20.0	15.5	0.0
975–1,149.99	2.1	4.1	20.2	26.4	3.3	32.6	8.3	2.9
1,150 and above	2.9	7.4	23.2	29.4	1.5	25.7	8.8	1.1
Total	2.5	4.3	21.1	28.8	6.5	25.4	9.3	2.0

Note: Each row adds up to 100 per cent.

activities and their accessibility to information on the availability of jobs. Keeping in view these two major factors, one model of occupational choice has been shifted. The appropriate framework for this purpose is the multinomial logit model. It has been attempted by considering both employment categories and occupational groups. However, due to the limited number of observations in some of the occupation groups such as transport, repairing, tailoring, professionals, and security (where there is no observation), the parameters for each of the occupation type, could not be estimated. Hence, we have been forced to combine some of the occupational groups. The new categories are as follows: (a) sales and trade (OCCP0), (b) manufacturing and repairing (OCCP1), (c) commercial services, tailoring, and professional jobs (OCCP2), (d) personal services (OCCP3), and (e) construction and transport (OCCP4).

It may be noted that the parameters from the multinomial logit model are directly not open to interpretation. This is because the parameters of one group are set to 0 while estimating the model in order to overcome the problem of indeterminacy. Nevertheless, the significance of the variables is examined, and marginal effects are calculated for interpretation.

The explanatory variables include continuous variables such as age (AGE), household size (HHSZ), and duration of migration (DMIG). The rest of the variables are in terms of dummies. EDUC is the dummy which makes a distinction between illiterates and those who are literates and who may have acquired higher education, i.e. EDUC takes a value of 0 and 1 respectively for these two groups. CAST stands for scheduled castes and scheduled tribes with a value of 1, and 0 otherwise. Those who reported to having property or cultivable land are differentiated from the rest by the dummy ASSET.

Three different kinds of networks are considered for understanding the role of informal channels through which workers gain access to information pertaining to the job market. NETWORK1 takes a value of 1 if workers accessed jobs through relatives, 0 otherwise. NETWORK2 makes a distinction between those who secured jobs through co-villagers/members of the same caste group/neighbours or co-inhabitants of the same cluster/friends, and the rest. NETWORK3 assigns a value of 1 if workers sought help from employers, NGOs, private contractors, or community leaders in getting jobs. The reference group comprises those who acquired jobs through self-efforts. In other words four categories of workers including those who made efforts by themselves to secure jobs, are identified; hence three network dummies are assigned.

We divided the city of Delhi into seven zones, and six zone-specific dummies (ZONEi, i=1–6) are included in the analysis to examine if different areas (zones) reveal differences in occupations or employment categories in which slum workers are engaged. Keeping in view the framework suggested in Section 2, both zone-specific and network dummies are crucial for our analysis.

First, we present the estimates of the multinomial logit model for workers divided on the basis of employment categories: (a) casual employment (EMP0), (b) regular-wage/salaried employment (EMP1), and (c) self-employment (EMP2). The comparison group in EMP2, i.e. in the process of estimation, the parameters for this group are set to 0. The MLE estimates of the parameters are reported in Table 7.10.

With an increase in household size women workers show a lower probability of joining casual employment relative to self-employment. Possibly the latter option offers them greater flexibility to combine household activities with work in the informal sector that adds to family income. The relatively younger people show a higher probability of securing casual employment as evident from the coefficient of age, which is negative. Scheduled castes are more likely to join casual jobs. Two network dummies (NETWORK2 and NETWORK3) are highly significant. In ZONE 1, ZONE 2, ZONE 3, and ZONE 5 women workers from slum households are largely engaged in casual jobs perhaps because such jobs are concentrated in these localities. With a rise in the duration of migration the probability of accepting casual employment seems to fall.

In getting regular-wage/salaried jobs NETWORK2 plays a significant role, suggesting the importance of contacts along the lines of caste, co-villagers, neighbours, and friends in the labour market. ZONE 4 shows a higher probability of joining regular-wage/salaried employment. Other variables are, however, mostly insignificant. In terms of marginal effects NETWORK3 shows a strong positive effect on casual employment. ZONES 1, 2, 3, and 5 are again found to raise the probability of casual employment. In regular-wage jobs NETWORK2 shows a net positive effect, and ZONE 6 is less likely to offer self-employment as seen from the marginal effects.

The analysis based on employment categories is too aggregative

TABLE 7.10: MAXIMUM LIKELIHOOD ESTIMATES OF THE MULTINOMIAL LOGIT MODEL: EMPLOYMENT CATEGORIES

	EMP0	EMP1
EDUC	0.50 (0.92)	-0.74 (-1.09)
HHSZ	-0.35 (-2.72)*	-0.21 (-1.35)***
CAST	1.40 (2.75)*	0.38 (0.65)
AGE	0.07 (2.50)*	0.03 (0.96)
ASSET	-0.32 (-0.50)	-0.42 (-0.58)
NETWORK1	1.04 (1.55)***	-0.28 (-0.33)
NETWORK2	2.52 (2.69)*	2.72 (2.86)*
NETWORK3	2.90 (2.56)*	0.39 (0.26)
ZONE1	3.27 (3.56)*	1.11 (1.06)
ZONE2	2.36 (2.94)*	2.95 (0.0001)
ZONE3	2.00 (2.07)*	1.11 (1.06)
ZONE4	1.60 (1.65)***	1.29 (1.91)**
ZONE5	1.97 (1.93)**	1.27 (1.10)
ZONE6	1.68 (1.30)***	1.26 (0.91)
DMIG	-0.19 (-1.87)**	-0.03 (-0.26)
Intercept	-1.70 (-1.11)	-0.86 (-0.50)

Chi-square = 104.56, which is significant at the 1 per cent level. N = 233.

Notes: (1) The comparison group is EMP2.

(2) The figures in parentheses are the t ratios. The asterisk marks *, **, and *** represent significance at the 5, 10, and 20 per cent levels respectively.

in nature in the sense that each category comprises several occupations, which are all highly heterogeneous. We, therefore, prefer to look carefully into the results based on occupation types. The comparison group, for which the parameters are set to 0 to avoid the problem of indeterminacy in a multinomial logit model, is OCCP2 (workers in commercial services, professional jobs, tailoring, etc.). The results are given in Table 7.11.

Age shows a negative effect on OCCP0 (occupation group comprising sales and trade divisions). Besides, CAST reduces the probability of employment in this occupation group though the coefficient is significant only at the 20 per cent level. Scheduled caste women are also less likely to get employment in manufacturing and repairing (OCCP1). NETWORK2 plays a significant role in accessing work opportunities in such occupations. With a rise in the duration of migration, the probability of getting employment in manufacturing and repairing increases. Household size also shows a

TABLE 7.11: MAXIMUM LIKELIHOOD ESTIMATES OF THE MULTINOMIAL LOGIT MODEL: OCCUPATION TYPES

	OCCP0	OCCP1	OCCP3	OCCP4
EDUC	-0.99 (-1.49)***	0.16 (0.23)	-0.67 (-1.32)000	-1.84 (-2.22)*
HHSZ	0.14 (0.15)	0.24 (1.42)***	-0.19 (-1.55)***	-0.09 (-0.55)
CAST	-0.95 (-1.50)***	-1.50 (-2.17)*	-0.52 (-1.04)	0.12 (0.17)
AGE	-0.06 (-1.91)**	-0.05 (-1.29)***	-0.03 (-1.36)***	-0.07 (-1.93)**
ASSET	0.16 (0.22)	-0.71 (-0.99)	0.22 (0.42)	-0.11 (-0.14)
NETWORK1	0.08 (0.11)	0.46 (0.49)	0.83 (1.40)***	0.53 (0.61)
NETWORK2	-3.50 (0.0001)	1.89 (1.80)**	2.14 (2.59)*	1.43 (1.83)**
NETWORK3	-0.49 (-0.59)	1.01 (1.16)	0.38 (0.63)	-1.09 (-0.91)
ZONE1	1.34 (1.79)**	-1.22 (-1.07)	2.81 (2.84)*	-0.13 (-0.10)
ZONE2	-0.93 (-0.55)	-2.71 (-1.89)**	0.65 (0.58)	-1.20 (-0.76)
ZONE3	1.59 (1.09)	-0.21 (-0.19)	1.86 (1.77)**	1.18 (1.89)**
ZONE4	2.12 (1.84)**	-0.15 (-0.12)	2.28 (1.91)**	1.42 (1.01)
ZONE5	0.22 (0.15)	-1.94 (-1.84)**	0.98 (0.94)	0.09 (0.07)
ZONE6	0.80 (0.50)	-0.61 (-0.46)	0.32 (0.24)	-3.70 (0.0001)
DMIG	0.14 (1.30)	0.24 (1.81)**	0.09 (1.16)	0.13 (1.10)
Intercept	0.26 (0.14)	0.30 (0.16)	0.04 (0.73)	1.67 (0.84)

Chi-square = 129.7, which is significant at the 1 per cent level. N = 233.

Notes: (1) OCCP2 is the comparison group.

(2) Same as note (2) of Table 7.10.

positive impact on it. Further, ZONES 2 and 5 are less likely to offer such jobs. On the other hand, ZONES 1, 3, and 4 seem to offer jobs in personal services (OCCP3) to a large extent. Again, NETWORK2 plays a significant role in accessing jobs of this type. NETWORK1 is also significant but only at 20 per cent level. Both age and household size reduce the probability of employment in personal services, though the coefficients are not significant at the 10 per cent level.

Illiterates show a higher probability of joining activities in the construction sector (OCCP4). Age again shows a negative effect, suggesting less scope for older women in such activities. NETWORK2 is somewhat significant only at the 20 per cent level. ZONE 3 seems to raise the probability of employment in the construction sector. On the other hand, ZONE 6 has a positive effect on employment in commercial services, etc. (OCCP2), as the estimate of marginal effects suggests.

On the whole, the access of women workers to the urban labour market is greatly influenced by the contacts they develop through co-villagers, neighbours/co-residents of the same cluster, friends, and members of the same caste group. Through these informal channels, operating mostly on the lines of ethnicity, they gain information regarding jobs and are absorbed in activities largely within the informal sector. Second, the findings tend to support the conclusion that different activities are concentrated in different areas within the city, suggesting that the city structure is highly heterogeneous in terms of the availability of jobs. The selection of activities from an individual point of view is supply driven. In other words, an entrant into the job market would like to get absorbed in a particular activity simply because of its availability in the area in which she resides. Though several other activities may be available in other parts of the city, workers, particularly women, would like to avail of only those which are adjacent to their place of residence. The zone-specific dummies are suggestive of such underlying influences characterizing the forces of demand and supply in the labour market.

7.5 Conclusion

In this chapter we observe that women workers in the urban informal sector are engaged mostly in the lower rungs of activities. Many of them come from large households, joining the labour market under economic compulsions. This is, of course, indicative of the double burden that they face in terms of managing a large household and simultaneously striving hard to augment the household income. Girls and elderly women do not seem to be largely present in the labour market, which could be due partly to the employers bias against the elderly women, and due partly to the under-reporting of the numbers and types of workers. Many women workers are either illiterates or just literates without any higher education. Casual jobs account for a significant proportion of total women employment, and in terms of occupation they are largely engaged in personal services. These are the activities which do not seem to facilitate skill formation and enhance their future status in the urban labour market that could potentially add to their bargaining strength, and raise the stream of future earnings. Hence, the scope for upward income mobility is quite limited for many of them. However, long duration migrants and the natives are relatively better off compared to the short and medium duration migrants as they manage to access jobs yielding higher earnings through their acquaintances. But the networks based on caste, friendship, and residence (same village of origin or same slum cluster in the city) are more important than the networks based on contacts with relatives, private contractors, NGOs, and community leaders. Ethnic bonds appear to be much stronger in this sense than the networks based on contacts with relatives.

Gender differentials in terms of income across most of the occupations are considerably high. An easy explanation is usually offered based on the skill or productivity differentials between the sexes. But within the informal sector many activities do not require highly skilled workers, and yet income differentials are high. This can partly be explained in terms of the bias of employers against women, whom they regard as being less productive and less reliable because of their responsibility to their household chores. But actually many women workers, due to shouldering the burden of household responsibilities, are not able to take up jobs on a full-time and regular basis, which leaves ample scope for employers to exploit them; part-timers possess weaker bargaining power compared to the full-timers. Often they are hard-pressed to combine multiple tasks on the home front, which would include cooking, cleaning, child care, collection of wood and drinking water, with several jobs in the informal sector, as revealed in several other studies (see Kalpagam, 2001). Consequently, with greater intensity of work they continue to receive low wages and by compensating others within the household in terms of consumption they eventually land up in lower expenditure size classes.

A more reasonable explanation for the low earnings of women workers is linked to their strong preference to work near their place of residence. The econometric analysis tends to substantiate this with the significance of the zone-specific dummies. Given the fact that not all activities are available in each of the areas within the city, a strong preference to work in the adjoining area increases the supply of labour more than proportionately for the activity that is located in the vicinity. And this, in turn, pulls the wages down. Since most of them operate through informal networks in accessing jobs, as the significance of the network dummy (NETWORK2) shows, the nature of jobs is unlikely to be widely different from that of the contact person. Hence, the situation of excess supply seems to be a persistent phenomenon in certain activities, particularly when we take a micro view of the city's economic and geographical structure. This, in turn, perpetuates the forces that entrap women workers in low-income employment, leaving them in a worse condition compared to their male counterparts in a similar position.

NOTES

1. The occupation groups are the same as given in Chapter 3.
2. The poverty line as per the modified expert group methodology is estimated at Rs. 309.5 in Delhi for the year 1993–4 (see Malhotra, 1997). When updated for the year 1999-2000 by the consumer price index for industrial workers in Delhi, the poverty live turns out to be Rs. 570 per month.

CHAPTER 8

POLICY REVIEW

The growing problem of slums and their impact on the larger society in terms of environmental pollution and increasing health hazards have been recognized by the planning authorities while laying down the social objectives in the plan documents. Nevertheless, it has also been recognized that housing is an endemic problem for millions of shelterless people. It has been emphasized that 'in India housing sector has always been given due importance in the development programme under the Five Year Plans', and that the provision of shelter is crucial to the development and improvement of the quality of life of the citizens.[1] In this wider context therefore, it is revelent to evaluate the programmes and measures undertaken so far to tackle the problems arising from the growth of slums. Moreover, the perception of the slum problem in the Indian context has to be emphasized before one may judge the appropriateness and effectiveness of policy divectives in reducing the intensity of the slum problem.

The earliest attempt made to provide public housing was the social housing scheme introduced in the First Five Year Plan. Thereafter, the integrated subsidized housing sector for industrial workers and the economically weaker sections (EWS) was introduced in 1952. The low-income group housing scheme (1954) and the middle income housing scheme (1959) were also undertaken subsequently. The first attack on the growth of slums was made in 1956, with the Slum Clearance Scheme or the Slum Area Act, 1956. But as a result of the recognition of the fact that the policy of slum clearance could not be successful in the face of the growing and seemingly intractable problem, the policy measures took a different turn—from clearance to improvement—following the recommendations of the Sixth Housing Ministers' Conference in 1962.[2]

It was then realized that the improvement of slums at site would be preferable to a policy of the relocation of slum dwellers and the construction of tenements and, therefore, the scheme for the environmental improvement of slums was formulated in 1972; the amenities to be provided under the scheme were water supply, sewerage, community baths and latrines, street lights, and the widening and paving of lanes.[3] During the Fifth Five Year Plan, in 1974, the scheme was transferred to the state sector as a part of the Minimum Needs Programme and it was intended to cover all cities with a population of above 3,00,000. The scope of the scheme was further widened in 1978 to cover all urban areas irrespective of the size of their populations.

In the Fifth Five Year Plan, the Integrated Urban Development Programme (IUDP), along with the Integrated Development of Small and Medium Towns (IDSMT), was introduced initially in the four metropolitan cities of Bombay, Calcutta, Delhi, and Madras. It was later extended to cover all towns with a view to providing assistance to the state governments to implement the land acquisition, development, and disposal programmes, urban renewal and redevelopment projects, and the provision of urban infrastructure. But when it was realized that the bulk of the resources were sanctioned simply for land acquisition, revised guidelines were issued in 1978 for providing water supply, sewerage, transportation facilities, and health facilities.[4] But as the report of the Task Force on Housing and Urban Development (1983) noted, the IUDP was not evaluated seriously.

The Sixth Five Year Plan also recognized the poor environmental and insanitary conditions in the slums and attached considerable importance to the programmes concerning the provision of basic amenities in the slum areas:

> A particular area becomes a slum not because of its structure but because of its environment and insanitation. Of the urban population nearly a fifth is estimated to constitute slum population. The slum population in 1985 needing attention is estimated to be about 33.1 million. Of this only 6.8 million have been covered by March 1980. It is proposed to cover about 40 per cent of the remaining slum population, that is 10 million slum population by 1985. Assuming per capita investment of Rs. 15.0 the total cost of this programme during the plan would be Rs. 15.1 crores. Depending on the strategy to be adopted in the area, facilities to be provided under the programme are water supply, storm water drains, paving of streets; street lighting and community latrines. Areas inhabited by scheduled castes are to be given top priority. (*Sixth Five Year Plan*, para 14.26, p. 225)

The Sixth Five Year Plan and the 20-Point Programme also accepted all the objectives of the International Year of Shelter for the

Homeless (IYSH). The United Nations Organization and the UN General Assembly proclaimed 1987 as the International Year of Shelter for the Homeless with a view to attracting the attention of the international community towards the need for providing shelter in the developed and developing countries. The main objective of the IYSH was to demonstrate policies and strategies for the improvement of shelter and the neighbourhoods of the poor and the disadvantaged by the year 1987 and to implement these policies and strategies so that benefits could accrue to all the world's homeless by the year 2000. However, the main requirement was that the governments of the different countries should ensure that the objectives of the IYSH were closely reflected in their policies and programmes and in this respect it was claimed in the booklet, *India and IYSH-1987*, that the Plan objectives in India were streamlined 'to reduce substantially the number of shelter-less people and to provide condition for others to improve their housing environment' (*SFYP*, para 23.11).[5]

On the whole, it appears that most of the policies and programmes formulated till at least the Sixth Five Year Plan revolved only around the issue of the housing shortage or the scarcity of shelter-cum-basic amenities. But even then they suffered from several major difficulties due to faulty land policy, shortage of resources, and, moreover, poor performance in the implementation of the objectives. The Study Group on Town Planning and Building Regulations appointed in 1981 (Ministry of Works and Housing) noted that the town planning acts combined with the land acquisition acts and the development authorities were basically oriented towards the preparation of master plans instead of anticipating planning at the regional or national level. The legislations dealing with town planning and the activities of the development authorities have, in fact, failed to provide a proper living environment, and in all the town planning areas the poorer sections suffered heavily because the land use controls, by creating different value systems, deprived them of access to the land.

Although there was a distinct shift of government policy in favour of providing basic infrastructure and of encouraging private initiative to construct the bulk of housing by themselves (*Task Forces*, 1983), several impediments relating to zoning regulations, standards of services, minimum plot sizes, maximum permissible density, requirements of minimum sizes of living spaces, and standards of building construction have discouraged the poor from making any significant investment (*Report of the Study Group*, 1981). The Task Forces on Housing and Urban Development (1983), realizing the problem of illegality, stated, 'There may indeed be the need in unsanitary, unsafe, pucca buildings but in hutments the problem is not bad sanitation alone but more importantly their illegality.'

The other aspects of the government programmes aimed at providing shelter and basic amenities to the urban poor can be judged from the performance of the resettlement colonies. Housing the slum dwellers in government-constructed tenements was both a complex and costly procedure, and, moreover, it could not be undertaken in the cities of Bombay and Calcutta where the scarcity of land seems to have been more acute. In Delhi, prior to 1970, 18 resettlement colonies were developed and between 1975–7 a further 15 locations were developed (Ribeiro, 1983). But as Rai (1985) notes, the old practice of the 1970s to shift squatters to specially constructed resettlement colonies was discontinued because of the heavy expenses involved.

The location of the new colonies also gave rise to certain major problems. It was felt that if newly constructed accommodation facilities were to be provided by the government then the slums should be removed to the outskirts of the cities instead of creating further congestion at the centre. But it seems difficult for the slum workers to reconcile to their new environment, as the income-earning opportunities are meagre in the new colonies compared to the crowded prosperous markets in the centre of the cities. In fact, the slum dwellers—working as porters, lifting loads in the grain markets or pulling rickshaws, and the female workers, cleaning utensils, or washing clothes, and the child workers, polishing shoes or supplying milk—are less likely to get any employment of the kind to which they are used in the new areas inhabited by the lower-income groups. On the other hand, after moving to the new colonies if they want to retain their market linkages at the old places of their work, the transport cost and duration of travel are likely to go up; these new burdens are particularly unacceptable to the female workers and the child workers.

Hence, the trade-off between the provision of better shelter-cum-basic amenities but with fewer employment opportunities, on the one hand, and the poor quality of the makeshift tenements but with better employment prospects, on the other, needs to be emphasized. It was found that in the capital city people had sold their plots in the resettlement colonies and were squatting once again on public land (Rai, 1985). The good-quality houses in these new resettlement colonies were in most cases owned by middle-class householders who purchased one or more plots from the original title holders. So the programme to provide shelter-cum-basic amenities seems to have involved certain major problems.

On the whole, until the Sixth Five Year Plan (1980–5) the urban policies mainly revolved around aspects of the housing-cum-basic amenities programme, including slum clearance and slum improvement, and upgradation, preparation of master plans, development of small and medium towns, strengthening of municipal civic administration, and so on. After the Sixth Plan the government measures may broadly be divided into two categories: (a) policies designed to improve the condition of housing and basic amenities in the slums, and (b) employment programmes. The Seventh Five Year Plan (1986-90) continued to lay emphasis on the Environment Improvement of Urban Slums (EIUS) scheme (started in 1974) and the Urban Basic Services (UBS) scheme (started in 1986). The scheme for Integrated Development of Small and Medium Towns (IDSMT) provided complementary infrastructural support to the towns. The provision of infrastructural facilities in the medium and small towns was expected to attract entrepreneurs and divert the investments away from the big cities. This, in turn, was expected to reduce the concentration of activities and population in the big cities. Further, the expansion of economic activities in small and medium towns was expected to divert the migrants away from the big cities. In addition to this, the Seventh Five Year Plan attached importance to (a) the provision of gainful employment to women and youth, (b) raising the earnings of those in low-paid jobs, and (c) stepping up the productivity and earnings of self-employed workers. However, it may be noted quite clearly that employment programmes have been launched only recently and that too on a limited scale. The Jawahar Rozgar Yojana with its three components—micro enterprises, wage employment, and shelter upgradation—was initiated only in 1989.

At the state level although there existed a few programmes, for example, Calcutta Metropolitan Development Authority's income support for slum dwellers; Madhya Pradesh Government's Training and Employment Programme for Urban Poor (STEPUP); and Tamil Nadu Slum Clearance Board's employment training for slum dwellers, the first central government scheme was formulated only in September 1986, i.e. the Self-Employment Programme for the

Urban Poor (SEPUP). Under this programme, workers in 35 economic activities (mostly in the services sector) such as hawking on handcart, laundering, welding, cycle rickshaw operation, shoe making, hair dressing, etc., with an income of Rs. 600 per month per household or less were supposed to get a loan of an amount not exceeding Rs. 5,000 per household. The impact of this programme was favourable although the income criterion, as pointed out by the National Commission on Urbanization (1988), was not fulfilled in 72 per cent of the cases as revealed by the differential rate of interest scheme (DRI), a programme quite similar to SEPUP. The commission (1988) noted that such programmes did not have a wide coverage mainly because they suffered from corruption and lack of publicity. It also noted that even the state-specific programmes, listed above, had a narrow coverage of only three lakh beneficiaries.

The National Commission on Urbanization (1988) came up with two sets of policy suggestions for improving the conditions of the urban poor and the slum dwellers: (i) Programme for Enhancement of Income and Employment Opportunities, and (ii) Extension of Basic Services. The former included: (a) National Programme of Employment Training for Urban Poor Youth, (b) National Programme of Credit Support for Assisting Micro-Enterprises for Technological Upgradation, (c) Micro-Enterprise Infrastructure Development Support, (d) Marketing Supports, and (e) New Programmes of Public Assets Creation for promoting wage employment for the urban poor. Although their suggestions are mainly aimed at augmenting the earnings of the informal sector workers, no mention has been made about raising the demand for informal activities either directly or through the inter-sectoral linkages.

The Commission also provided a list of cities and towns (called Generating Economic Momentum–GEMS), which should get much attention in the development plans. These cities or towns are said to possess the potential for development in terms of their existing industrial base. Besides, some of these cities/towns are already or were once the state capitals and business centres. Some of the district headquarters have also been included in this list. Development of infrastructure is likely to expand economic activities in these cities and towns, which, in turn, would, it was hoped, moderate the population pressure in the million-plus cities.

Keeping in view the importance of some of the employment schemes introduced in the Seventh Five Year Plan (1986-90) and the suggestions made by the National Commission on Urbanization (1988), the Eighth Five Year Plan (1992–7) laid considerable emphasis on the generation of adequate employment, the containment of population growth through the active cooperation of people, and the provision of safe drinking water and primary health care facilities. It also aimed at developing the small and medium towns. In fact, the concept of GEMS as identified by the National Commission on Urbanization (1988) had been considered for implementation. It also emphasized that 'programmes to deal with the problem of urban poverty should be developed in an integrated manner emphasizing both employment generation and access to basic services involving community level organization' (*Eighth Five Year Plan*, 1992–7, vol. II, p. 352). Considerable emphasis was laid on the Jawahar Rozgar Yojana and the existing schemes of the Self-Employment Programme for Urban Poor (SEPUP). The Scheme Self-Employment for Educated Unemployed Youth (SEEUY) was proposed to be implemented on a large scale. It also aimed at introducing a wage policy in the urban informal sector for reducing the differences in the earning in the formal and informal sectors. However, the enforcement of the minimum-wage legislation is difficult to implement in the informal sector partly because of the heterogeneous nature of this sector. Second, such a policy would reduce the wage employment in this sector. On the other hand, informal sector earnings may be promoted through improvement in demand.

The Ninth Plan also noted that the problem of urban poverty was due to the lack of productive employment and thus income, high rate of inflation, and inadequacy of social infrastructure, all of which affect both the quality of life of the individuals and their employability. Some programmes which have been launched recently or which have been given a new orientation to provide more opportunities to involve the poor in the economic process are as follows.

The urban poverty alleviation programmes such as the Jawahar Rozgar Yojana, Urban Basic Services for the Poor, and the Prime Minister's Integrated Urban Poverty Eradication Programme were all included in the Swarna Jayanti Shahari Rozgar Yojana (SJSRY), which was launched in December 1997. This scheme has two components: (a) the Urban Self Employment Programme (USEP), and (b) the Urban Wage Employment Programme (UWEP). The first component, that is, the self-employment programme comprised three major categories: (i) assistance to individual urban poor beneficiaries for setting up gainful self-employment ventures; (ii) assistance to groups of urban poor women for setting up gainful self-employment ventures under the scheme for development of women and children in the urban areas (DWCUA); and (iii) training of beneficiaries, potential beneficiaries, and other persons associated with the urban employment programme for the upgradation and acquisition of vocational and entrepreneurial skills. The USEP seeks to provide wage employment to beneficiaries living below the poverty line by utilizing their labour for the construction of socially and economically useful public assets. The outlay for the SJSRY in the Ninth Plan was Rs. 1,009 crores. The actual expenditure during 1997–8 was Rs. 102.51 crores as against an approved outlay of Rs. 188 crores. During the year 1998–9, the revised estimate was Rs. 162.28 crores as compared to a provision of Rs. 188.50 crores. For the Annual Plan 1999–2000 an outlay of Rs. 180.65 crores was earmarked (Annual Plan, 1999–2000).

The other support mechanism that exists for the urban poor is the public distribution system (PDS), though it has been widely criticized for its failure to serve the population below the poverty line. A detailed assessment of the PDS is given in Kundu (1993). The Basic Minimum Services (BMS) programme, which was launched in 1996 on the recommendations of the Conference of Chief Ministers, adopted the following objectives: (a) 100 per cent coverage of provision of safe drinking water in rural and urban areas; (b) 100 per cent coverage of primary health facilities in rural and urban areas; (c) universalization of primary education; (d) provision of public housing assistance to all shelterless poor families; (e) provision of connectivity to all unconnected villages and habitations; (f) extension of the midday meal programme in primary schools to all rural blocks and urban slums and disadvantaged sections; and (g) the streamlining of the public distribution system with a focus on the poor.

Although the issue of employment in the urban context has been given importance in recent years, much more needs to be done at the ground level. The share of urban informal sector employment is on the rise (Mitra, 2001a), and second, the employment schemes have not been implemented on any large scale in all categories of cities and towns. The framework of policy for dealing with this sector has to recognize its vast heterogeneity. The growing needs of skill development, technology transfer, and the marketing of products of this sector are to be given priority in order to upgrade this sector. This, however, needs to be done without trying to convert the informal secotor into the formal sector; the elements of informality which often encourage employment growth in this sector need to be retained while trying to improve the productivity levels (Bhargava, 2001). An important conclusion which follows from our analysis is that poor/low-income households themselves are actively involved in improving their conditions, and in their attempts to do so they try to take advantage of all resources and networks that are available to them. Even the biggest investors in low-income housing are the poor themselves, as noted by the *Global Report on Human Settlements* (2001); they manage to arrive in the city with their limited resources, invest in housing, negotiate for services, and secure land tenure. The policy directives need to recognize some of these efforts, which not only would reduce the burden on the public exchequer but which would also deal with the problems of slums, basic amenities, and poverty more efficiently. Instead of the government being always directly involved in the process of employment generation in the informal sector on a large scale, measures to protect and support the efforts made by the low-income households can be pursued to enable them to attain their goals.

The interdependencies between poverty, availability of amenities, and the quality of life have been analysed by Kundu (2001) based on the state level data from various rounds of the NSSO's surveys on consumption expenditure, housing, and other amenities. He argues that a large majority of the poor are not located in slum areas or in non-*pucca* houses, though that is the conventional notion the planners usually have. Hence, basic amenities and support programmes for employment generation must not remain confined only to slums. The intra-city variation in the level and quality of amenities is high and increasing over time as the ward level data available from the Population Censuses indicate (Kundu, 2001). High-income areas have been selected by the private entrepreneurs for the provision of high-quality amenities, while the slum areas and poor households continue to have inadequate access to drinking water and sanitation. It is not true that they cannot afford to pay the user charges, but the capital expenditure involved in obtaining a new water connection or toilet facility is exorbitantly high. Some of these issues need to be attended to immediately by the policy makers.

NOTES

1. Buta Singh (Minister, Works and Housing, Parliamentary Affairs and Sports): Preface to the booklet *India and IYSH-1987*, Government of India, 1987.
2. Meera Bapat, 'Slum Areas Legislation: Its Relevance for Slum Improvement and Upgradation', Task Forces on Housing and Urban Development, Planning Commission, Government of India, Paper 5.6, New Delhi, 1983.
3. Ribeiro (1983).
4. Task Forces on Housing and Urban Development, Part IV, Shelter for the Urban Poor, Planning Commission, Government of India, New Delhi, 1983.
5. *India and IYSH-1987*, Government of India, New Delhi, 1987.

CHAPTER 9

CONCLUSION

This study focuses on issues that relate to micro responses to macro economic changes which are responsible for the growth of city slums and examines the efforts made by their inhabitants to escape poverty. It reveals the interplay between the forces of indivisibilities, infrastructure and the concentration of activities, on the one hand, and, on the other, individual preferences for occupations and locations, and individual endowments and attributes such as education, assets and networks. Instead of succumbing to the poor socio-economic conditions in which they live, the low-income households develop strategies to cope with the uncertainties they face. These strategies are significant not only for analytical purposes but also for policy making. A study such as this enables one to perceive the measures that attribute merit to individual responses and complements them in attaining individual goals. Without a profound understanding of their behaviour mere discussions of the growth or anti-poverty measures at the level of the aggregate economy are bound to be futile. This belief prompted the present study to focus on occupational choice and the role of networks in accessing information pertaining to the urban labour market, the extent of upward income mobility, the contribution of women to the household economy through labour market participation notwithstanding the discrimination they face, the standards of living and health conditions, and individual actions based on altruism and/or exchange. The study is based on a micro survey carried out during 1999–2000 in the slums of Delhi. The survey followed a random sampling technique and covered around 800 slum households located in different parts of the city.

Urbanization is expected to offer employment opportunities to the members of the low-income households who migrate in search of jobs from the rural areas. Information, skill, and experience then facilitate the process of upward income mobility. However, given the diverse nature of the city's economic structure and the variations in economic activities conducted across space, individual preferences for occupations based on their social and economic asset base and their urge to reside near the work place often increase the pressure on land and housing. Hence, slums and squatters are an inevitable part of the urbanization process. Since slum demolition is an impossible alternative particularly in a democratic society, appropriate policy formulation to tackle these issues is an integral part of urban planning and urban development. Some of the factors such as industrialization, expansion of the rural non-farm sector and the urban informal sector, and political support that explain the growth of slums are listed in Chapter 2.

Chapter 3 deals with occupation, network, and the physical segmentation of the urban labour market and reveals the associations among occupation groups (employment categories) and several individual attributes such as gender, caste, education, migration status, assets, networks, and the preference to reside near the work place. The various types of informal and formal channels of information flow that exist in the society pertaining to the urban labour market determine the ultimate selection of occupation. While certain occupations are accessed largely through relatives—general as well as close—certain others are accessed through co-villagers, friends, neighbours, and members of the same caste groups, and some others are secured through formal channels such as NGOs and employment exchange. On the whole, there seems to be a relationship between the nature of occupations and the nature of networks given the impact of factors such as caste, gender, migration status, and education. The nature of networks changes over time with the acquisition of experience, which again facilitates the process of upward mobility. There is evidence of improvement in the levels of income, accompanied by the changes in the nature of networks and occupations, as noted in Chapter 4. Though the graduation hypothesis from the informal sector to the formal sector does not seem to be substantiated by evidence, even within the informal sector workers are found to change occupations, and this, in turn, adds to their benefits. Chapter 4 reveals that in the initial stages networks are of great significance, but for those who had already been in urban jobs earlier self-efforts are important to secure any further improvement in occupation and income.

The significance of the zone-specific dummies examined in Chapter 3 is suggestive of the diverse economic structure existing in the city, supporting the physical segmentation of the urban labour market. Though from the macro point of view unlimited supplies of labour are taken to exist almost as a certainty, a closer look at the survey data allows us to dispel the illusion that often surrounds our understanding of urban development. Intra-city variations in activities explain variations in employment opportunities across space, and consequently the impact on housing and other basic amenities leading to over congestion in certain localities. That workers in only certain occupations are predominantly present in specific localities, as evident from the zone dummies, tends to provide indirect support to the view regarding the preference of individuals to reside in close proximity to the work place, which, in turn, explains the physical segmentation of the urban labour market. That not all slums are of the same type, and that the problems the inhabitants face could be quite diverse in nature are conclusions borne out by such patterns. Though some of the problems relating to basic amenities could largely be an endemic feature of most of the slums, individual responses to the challenges that the inhabitants face and the efforts they make to overcome them could be significantly different. Hence, policy directives need to consider these realities.

Though one would expect a high incidence of poverty to occur among the slum dwellers, findings from the chapter on living standards do not suggest this. However, a closer look at the data tells us that the percentage of the population just marginally above the poverty line is quite large. With an increase in the income of the household head the standard of living in terms of per capita expenditure improves. Given the percentage of children within the household, any increase in the household size, implying an increase due to the increase in the number of adults, tends to improve the quality of housing. However, with an increase in the proportion of children the per capita expenditure increases instead of declining though the latter case is usually expected. The increase could be due to the contribution made by child labour in augmenting the family income and thus the expenditure in per capita terms. Relationships between occupations and/or employment categories and standards of living are noteworthy, and hence it would be misleading to characterize all activities within the informal sector by low productivity. It is quite evident that female-headed households are worse off compared to the male-headed households in terms of per capita consumption expenditure. The significance of the zone-specific dummies, particularly in the equations for the quality of housing, again indicates the heterogeneity in living standards interspatially. Even in terms of the per capita consumption expenditure some of the zones turn out to have lower living standards compared to the rest. However, even within these so-called low-income households variations in living standards exist as their resources and responses to challenges vary. The effect of caste on the quality of housing is not insignificant either; the scheduled castes usually reside in poor-quality housing. The impact of education on both quality of housing and per capita expenditure is positive. Some of these findings along with interconnections between health and per capita expenditure have important policy implications.

Addressing ourselves to the larger issues of individual behaviour in understanding the practice of networks, we analysed whether transfers—monetary and non-monetary both—are motivated by the feeling of altruism or exchange. Notwithstanding the limitations of the data, the empirical results tend to suggest that the monetary/non-monetary help given is dependent on the help received from others. In other words, it appears to be an act of reciprocation. Hence, interpreting remittances purely on the basis of altruism may not be correct. Other factors that matter in determining transfers are education, caste, household size, ability to save, contact with the place of origin, the duration of migration, and stability of the job market. Holding property at and visits to the place of origin influence the decision to remit, which is indicative of the practice of exchange, though in its face value altruism seems to be the motivating factor. With an increase in the duration of migration people tend to remit more because their ability to earn as well as to save increases over time and with experience. However, the other side of the story also needs to be understood. With an increase in experience in urban labour market the ability to help others in accessing jobs also increases, and hence more relatives and co-villagers of the first-comers are expected to migrate to the city. As this may dampen the future earnings of the first-comers in the urban labour market due to the rise in the supplies of labour, and also increase their liabilities on the domestic front—for they may have to put up the newcomers in their own households—remittances are considered to be better and more effective substitutes. Networks which are in wide practice for accessing information on the job market are also, in fact, indicative of mutual help—emphasizing the principle of exchange rather than altruism—though the nature of reciprocation need not be the same.

Chapter 7 discusses gender issues, and it is observed that women workers in the urban informal sector are engaged mostly in the lower rungs of activities. Many women working in the informal sector seem to come from large households, which is indicative of the double burden they face in managing a large household and struggling to augment the household income. Many women workers are either illiterates or just literates without any higher education, being employed in casual jobs in personal services. These activities do not seem to facilitate skill formation and enhance their future status in the urban labour market. But migrants who have been staying in the city for long and the natives compared to the short- and medium-duration migrants are relatively better off as they manage to access jobs yielding higher earnings through their acquaintances. Income differentials across sexes in most of the occupations are considerably high. Even when skill requirements are not high, income differentials between the sexes exist. This could be because many of the women workers, due to household responsibilities, are not able to take up jobs on a full-time and regular basis, which leaves ample scope for employers to exploit them. As a result with greater intensity of work they continue to receive low wages and by compensating others within the household in terms of consumption they land up in lower expenditure size classes. As they largely prefer to work in the vicinity of their households, which is evident from the significance of the zone dummies, at times supplies of labour in certain activities exceed demand to a great extent, which in turn perpetuates the forces that entrap women workers in low-income jobs.

Finally, Chapter 8 reviews the policy measures, and highlights the inadequacy of government policies to generate employment for the urban poor. Most attempts revolve around the issue of housing and basic amenities though in recent years the importance of employment issues has been increasingly recognized. Supportive measures rather than direct interventions are seen to be both cost-effective and promising. Direct interventions which include slum demolition and rehabilitation, banning entry to the city without prior approval from the government, and forced rural diversification may turn out to be highly expensive. Supportive measures on the other hand tend to supplement the existing informal mechanism of networks and exchange instead of conflicting with them. Such measures include provision of basic amenities like sanitation, drinking water, health care, assistance to NGOs and local authorities to disseminate job information and run educational and training institutions—which can help skill formation and facilitate upward mobility—and provision of micro credit to enterprises in the urban informal sector. Individuals efforts to improve the shelter conditions can be strengthened by providing inexpensive housing loans through NGOs, etc. The combined capabilities and strengths of governments at various levels, market mechanisms, and civil society networks need to be considered by the new forms of governance. Such governance would develop, as the *Global Report on Human Settlements* (2001) highlights, the unrealized productive potential of the poor and help enhance social harmony by making policies supportive of the poor and at the same time beneficial to the rest of the society. Second, as highlighted in our analysis, the heterogeneity of slums even within a particular city and the variations in terms of the problems that slum residents face need to be given due consideration in framing policies for urban development.

BIBLIOGRAPHY

Acharya, Sarthi and Arup Mitra, 'The Potential of Rural Industries and Trade to Provide Decent Work Conditions: A Data Reconnaissance in India', ILO-SAAT Working Paper, New Delhi, 2000.

Agarwal, Bina, *A Field of One's Own: Gender and Land Rights in South Asia*, Cambridge: Cambridge University Press, 1994.

Banerjee, Biswajit, 'Some Aspects of Rural-Urban Migration in India: A Case Study of Delhi', unpublished Ph.D. thesis, Oxford: University of Oxford, 1981.

———, 'The Role of the Informal Sector in the Migration Process: A Test of Probabilistic Migration Models and Labour Market Segmentation for India', *Oxford Economic Papers*, vol. 35, 1983.

———, 'Information Flow, Expectations and Job Search: Rural to Urban Migration Process in India', *Journal of Development Economics*, vol. 15, 1984.

———, *Rural to Urban Migration and the Urban Labour Market*, Himalaya Publishing House, 1986.

———, 'The Determinants of Migrating with a Pre-Arranged Job and of the Initial Duration of Urban Unemployment: An Analysis Based on Indian Data on Rural-to-Urban Migrants', *Journal of Development Economics*, vol. 36, 1991.

Banerjee, Biswajit and Gabriella A. Bucci, 'On the Job Search after Entering Urban Employment: An Analysis Based on Indian Migrants', *Oxford Bulletin of Economics and Statistics*, vol. 56, no. 1, 1994.

Banerjee, Biswajit and S.M. Kanbur, 'On the Specification and Estimation of Macro Rural-Urban Migration Functions: With an Application to Indian Data', *Oxford Bulletin of Economics and Statistics*, vol. 43, no.1, 1981.

Banerjee, Biswajit and J.B. Knight, 'Caste Discrimination in the Indian Urban Labour Market', *Journal of Development Economics*, vol. 17, 1985.

Banerjee, N., 'How Real is the Bogy of Feminization'? *The Indian Journal of Labour Economics*, vol. 40, no. 3, 1997.

Bharat Sevak Samaj, Delhi, *Slum of Old Delhi*, 1958.

Bhargava, Gopal, *Development of India's Urban Rural and Regional Planning in 21st Century: Policy Perspective*, New Delhi: Gyan Publishing House, 2001.

Chopra, Kanchan, 'Social Capital and Development Processes: Role of

Formal and Informal Institutions', *Economic and Political Weekly*, 13 July 2002.

Datta-Chaudhuri, M., 'Infrastructure and Location', in John Cody, H. Hughes and D. Wall (eds.), *Policies for Industrial Progress in Developing Countries*, New York: Oxford University Press, 1980.

Datta-Chaudhury, Tamal, 'A Theoretical Analysis of the Informal Sector', *World Development*, vol. 17, no. 3, 1989.

Dreze, Jean and A.K. Sen, *Hunger and Public Action*, London: Oxford University Press, 1989.

Deshpande, Sudha, 'Impact of Emerging Labour Market on Women and Their Households: A Tale of Three Slums in Mumbai', in A. Kundu and A.N. Sharma (eds.), *Informal Sector in India: Perspectives and Policies*, New Delhi: Institute for Human Development and Institute of Applied Manpower Research, 2001.

Dupont, V., 'Mobility Patterns and Economic Strategies of Houseless People in Old Delhi', in V. Dupont, E. Tarlo and Denis Vidal (eds.), *Urban Space and Human Destinies*, New Delhi: Manohar, 2000.

Dupont, V. and Arup Mitra, 'Population Distribution, Growth and Socio-Economic Spatial Patterns in Delhi: Findings from the 1991 Census Data,' *Demography India*, vol. 24, no 1, 1995.

Fallon, Peter R., 'Education and the Duration of Job Search and Unemployment in Urban India: An Empirical Analysis Based on a Survey of Jobseekers', *Journal of Development Economics*, vol. 12, 1983.

Global Report on Human Settlements, *Cities in a Globalizing World*, United Nations Centre for Human Settlements (Habitat), London: Earthscan Pub. Ltd., 2001.

Government of India, *Task Forces on Housing and Urban Development* (in four parts), New Delhi, Planning Commission, 1983.

———, *Eighth Five Year Plan 1992–7*, vols. I and II, New Delhi: Planning Commission, 1992.

———, *Annual Plan, 1999–2000*, New Delhi: Planning Commission, 1999–2000.

Gupta, Indrani and Arup Mitra, 'Child Labour: A Profile of Delhi Slums', *Indian Journal of Labour Economics*, vol. 40, no. 4, Oct.–Dec. 1997.

Harris, J.R. and M.P. Todaro, 'Migration, Unemployment and Development: A Two Sector Analysis', *American Economic Review*, vol. LX, no. 1, 1970.

Hemmer, H. and C. Mannel, 'On the Economic Analysis of the Urban Informal Sector', *World Development*, vol. 17, no. 10, 1989.

Henderson, J.V., 'Efficiency of Resource Usage and City Size', Journal of Urban Economics, vol. 19, no. 1, 1986.

———, Urban Development: Theory, Fact and Illusion, New York: Oxford University Press, 1988.

Hermansen, Tormod, 'Development Poles and Related Theories: A Synotic Review', in N.M. Hansen (ed.), *Growth Centres in Regional Economic Development*, New York: The Free Press, 1972.

Hirway, Indira, 'Review Paper on Impact of Anti Poverty Programmes on Women', National Commission on Self-Employed Women, New Delhi: Government of India, 1987.

Hoselitz, B., 'The Role of Cities in the Economic Growth of Underdeveloped Countries', *Journal of Political Economy*, vol. 61, no. 3, 1953.

———, 'Generative and Parasitic Cities', *Economic Development and Cultural Change*, vol. 3, no. 3, 1955.

———, 'Urbanisation and Economic Growth in Asia', *Economic Development and Cultural Change*, vol. 6, no. 1, 1957.

Institute of Social Studies Trust, 'Role of the Informal Service in Poverty Alleviation in India', Report prepared for the United Nations Economic and Social Commission for Asia and the Pacific, Bangkok, 1997.

International Labour Office, *Towards Full Employment: A Programme for Columbia*, Geneva: ILO, 1970.

———, *Employment, Incomes and Equality: A Strategy for Increasing Productive Employment in Kenya*, Geneva: ILO, 1972.

Kalpagam, U., 'Globalisation, Liberalisation and Women Workers in the Informal Sector', in A. Kundu and A.N. Sharma (eds.), *Informal Sector in India: Perspectives and Policies*, New Delhi: Institute for Human Development and Institute of Applied Manpower Research, 2001.

Kannapan, S., 'Employment Problem and the Urban Labour Market in Developing Nations', *Economic Development and Cultural Change*, vol. 33, no. 4, 1983.

Kundu, Amitabh, *Urban Development and Urban Research in India*, New Delhi: Khama Publishers, 1992.

———, *In the Name of the Urban Poor: Access to Basic Amenities*, New Delhi: Sage Publications India Pvt. Ltd., 1993.

———, 'Trends and Structure of Employment in the 1990s: Implications for Urban Growth', *Economic and Political Weekly*, 14 June 1997.

———, 'Access of Urban Poor to Housing Amenities: Aspects Concerning Social Security', in S. Mahendra Dev et al. (eds.), *Social and Economic Security in India*, New Delhi: Institute for Human Development, 2001.

Kuznets, S., *Modern Economic Growth: Rate, Structure, and Spread*, New Haven: Yale University Press, 1966.

Lauby, Jennifer and Oded Stark, 'Individual Migration as a Family Strategy: Young Women in the Philippines', *Population Studies*, vol. 42, 1988.

Lewis, W. A., 'Economic Development with Unlimited Supplies of Labour', The Manchester School of Economic and Social Studies, 1954.

Lipton, Michael, *Why Poor People Stay Poor*, London: Temple Smith, 1980.

Lucas, Robert E.B. and Oded Stark, 'Motivations to Remit: Evidence from Botswana', *Journal of Political Economy*, vol. 93, 1985.

Malhotra, Rajeev, 'Incidence of Poverty in India: Towards a Consensus on Estimating the Poor', *Indian Journal of Labour Economics*, vol. 40, no. 1, 1997.

Miller, B.D., *The Endangered Sex: Neglect of Female Children in Rural North India*, Ithaca, NY: Cornell University Press, 1981.

Mills, Edwin S. and Arup Mitra, *Urban Development and Urban Ills*, New Delhi: Commonwealth Publishers, 1997.

Mills, E.S. and C. Becker, *Studies in Indian Urban Development*, A World Bank Research Publication, Oxford University Press, 1986.

Mills, E.S. , 'An Aggregate Model of Resource Allocation in a Metropolitan Area', *American Economic Review*, vol. 57, 1967.

Mitra, Arup, 'Government Policy for Slum Improvement', *Mainstream*, 19 July 1986.

———, 'Spread of Slums: The Rural Spill-Over?', *Demography India*, vol. XVII, no. 1, 1988.

———, 'Duality, Employment Structure and Poverty Incidence: Slum Perspective', *Indian Economic Review*, vol. XXV, no. 1, 1990.

———, 'Urban Poverty: A Rural Spill-over?', *Indian Economic Review*, Special Number in Memory of Sukhamoy Chakravarty, vol. 27, 1992.

———, 'Rural Non-Farm Employment, Poverty and Women', *Indian Journal of Labour Economics*, Special Issue on Non-Farm Sector, G.K. Chadha (ed.), vol. 36, no. 3, 1993.

———, *Urbanisation, Slums, Informal Sector Employment and Poverty: An Exploratory Study*, Delhi: B.R. Publishing Corporation, 1994.

———, 'National Report: India', in *Survey Report: Changing Labour Market and Women Employment*, Tokyo: Asian Productivity Organisation, 2000.

———, 'Urban Labour Market in India: An Overview', *International Journal of Employment Studies*, vol. 9, no. 2, 2001a.

———, 'Employment in the Informal Sector', in A. Kundu and A.N. Sharma (eds.), *Informal Sector in India: Perspectives and Policies*, Delhi: Institute for Human Development and Institute of Applied Manpower Research, 2001b.

Mohan, Rakesh, *Urban Economic and Planning Models*, Baltimore, MD: Johns Hopkins University Press, 1979.

Moser, C.O.N., 'Gender Planning in the Third World: Meeting Practical and Strategic Gender Needs', *World Development*, vol. 17, no. 11, 1989.

Mukhopadhyay, Swapna, 'Locating Women within Informal Sector Hierarchies', in T.S. Papola and A.N. Sharma (eds.), *Gender and Employment in India*, New Delhi: Vikas Publishing House, 1999.

National Institute of Urban Affairs, *Women in the Urban Informal Sector*, Research Study Series, no. 49, 1991.

Papola, T.S., 'Rural Industrialisation and Agricultural Growth: A Case Study on India', in R. Islam (ed.), *Rural Industrialisation and Employment in Asia*, New Delhi: ILO/ARTEP, 1987.

———, *Urban Informal Sector in a Developing Economy*, New Delhi: Vikas Publishing House, 1981.

Patrick, Martin, 'Unorganised Women in an Urban Setting: Opportunities and Challenges', in A. Kundu and A.N. Sharma (eds.), *Informal Sector in India: Perspectives and Policies*, Delhi: Institute for Human Development and Institute of Applied Manpower Research, 2001.

Rai, Usha, 'Beyond the Reach of the Law', *The Times of India*, New Delhi: 19 July 1985.

Rebeiro, E.F.N., 'Planning for the Urban Poor: Basic Needs and Priorities', in A.D'Souza (ed.), *Urban Growth and Urban Planning*, Indian Social Institute, 1983.

Report of the National Commission on Urbanisation, Government of India, 1988.

Sethuraman, S.V., 'The Urban Informal Sector: Concept, Measurement and Policy', *International Labour Review*, vol. 114, no. 1, 1976.

Sharma, A.N. and S. Singh (eds.), *Women and Work: Changing Scenario in India*, Delhi: B.R. Publishing Corporation, 1993.

Shukla, V., 'Rural Non-Farm Activity: A Regional Model and its Empirical Application to Maharashtra,' *Economic and Political Weekly*, 9 November 1991.

Singh, A.M. and A. D'Souza, *The Urban Poor: Slum and Pavement Dwellers in the Major Cities of India*, New Delhi: Manohar, 1980.

Standing, Guy, 'Urban Workers and Patterns of Employment', in S. Kannappan (ed.), *Studies of Urban Labour Market Behaviour in Developing Areas*, Geneva: International Institute for Labour Studies, 1977.

Standing, H., *Dependence and Autonomy: Women's Employment and the Family in Calcutta*, London: Routledge, 1991.

Stark, Oded, 'On Modelling the Informal Sector', *World Development*, vol. 10, no. 5, 1982.

———, 'Altruism and the Quality of Life', *American Economic Review* (Papers and Proceedings), vol. 79, 1989.

———, *Altruism and Beyond: An Economic Analysis of Transfers and Exchanges within Families and Groups*, Cambridge: Cambridge University Press, 1995.

———, and Robert E.B. Lucas, 'Migration, Remittances, and the Family', *Economic Development and Cultural Change*, vol. 36, 1988.

Tinker, I. (ed.), *Persistent Inequalities: Women and World Development*, New York: Oxford University Press, 1990.

Todaro, M.P., 'A Model of Labour Migration and Urban Unemployment in Less Developed Countries', *American Economic Review*, vol. LIX, no. 1, 1969.

Tokman, Victor E., 'Policies for a Heterogeneous Informal Sector in Latin America, *World Development*, vol. 17, no. 7, 1989.

Williamson, J.G., 'Migration and Urbanisation', in H. Chenery and T.N. Srinivasan (eds.), *Handbook of Development Economics*, vol. 1, Amsterdam: Elsevier Science Publishers, 1988.

INDEX